Taste
and
Savor

Delicious
Healthy Recipes
and
Tasty Wine Tips

Nancy Waldeck

Library of Congress Cataloging-in-Publication Data Atlanta, Georgia

First edition
Index
Taste and Savor, Heathy Recipes, Wine Tips
ISBN: 978-0-615-41425-6

Introduction

This book is the result of a whim. In the fall of 2007, I decided
to start sharing some of my recipes and wine tips with a small
group of friends over the Internet. I wanted it to reflect my cooking
philosophy, so I designed a colorful one-pager, simple to read,
with quick "eating better" recipes and straightforward wine tips.
I published the first Friday Four with a recipe for roasted
tomatoes and hit the button to send. Little did I know that
3 years later, I would have thousands of readers from all over
the globe, anticipating my recipe and wine pairings each week.

As time passed, I discovered that many home cooks have
printed and kept the recipes in a kitchen file for quick reference.
When I was talking to my friend Caroline about writing a cookbook,
her first response was, "please, please give us a Friday Four book
so I can quickly access the recipes by type".

So, for all you Friday Four followers, here it is: a compilation
of some of my favorite recipe and wine pairings. I hope you enjoy
this book as much as I have loved meeting you through food
and wine delivered to your inbox each week. And for those of you
who are not subscribers, here's your introduction to the fun
and adventure of new recipes and delicious wine in the Friday Four
e-zine. We hope you will become part of our intrepid cooking and
tasting group, too!

Contents:

Food Words

Good Food doesn't need to be hard. I love to eat, and I bet you do too.
We all want to enjoy food, but the never-ending conflict between time,
creativity and information sometimes makes even dinner tonight difficult!
The recipes presented here require little previous cooking experience
and take little time - some may seem familiar and some may be new
to you. But whether new or familiar, each one has been translated into
better-for-you eating, with easy, step-by-step directions and explanations.

Any kitchen technique, tip, trick or ingredient that may be unfamiliar are
explained with a *Kitchen Smidgen*.

A *Get Creative* Idea gives suggestions about how to use your newfound
food knowledge. If you run across ingredients that you don't recognize, no
worries. I've added them to ramp up the flavor and nutrition of a recipe,
and all are conveniently available in the supermarket, big box stores,
local international markets or online. In addition, the appendix lists these
ingredients to make shopping easier.

My hope is that the recipes and wine ideas will empower you to be
healthier and happy in the kitchen. For me food is an expression of love,
and the sharing of it is a way to show others just how important they are.
Please use this book as a guide to making your food better for you,
more creative, more flavorful and packed with energy for life.

Guide to Using This Book

✤ ## *Kitchen Smidgen*
Kitchen techniques, tips, tricks or ingredients used in the
recipe that may be unfamiliar or side suggestions that are
delicious accompaniments.

✤ ## get creative
How to use ingredients or kitchen tools in a creative new way.

🍇 ## Tasty Wine Tips
Wines that perfectly pair with each recipe and are widely available.

🍅 ## *Vegetarian*
This recipe includes only vegetables.

🦞 ## *Pescetarian*
This recipe includes fish and shellfish.

🐓 ## *Flexitarian*
This recipe includes meat or poultry.

📺 ## *Taste and Savor TV*
Find information about the techniques and ingredients in this recipe on
Taste and Savor TV at http://www.youtube.com/user/tasteandsavortv

Please note: The recipes in the book serve from 6 – 8 diners, depending on whether you
serve them as an appetizer, main or side. I've used TB as the abbreviation for Tablespoon
and Tsp as the abbreviation for Teaspoon.

Some Wine Tips as you Taste through the Book

Don't let anyone scoff at your wine reflections or your choices! Be vocal and bold. Try to associate your aromas and tastes concretely and in a way that others can understand. For instance, say that a wine "smells like flowers" instead of "the aroma of my mother's perfume". We all have a general understanding of a floral fragrance – but not the particular aroma of your lovely mother.

Temperature is important. If you are looking for a way to enjoy and learn about all the subtle nuances of wine. Don't drink your red wine too warm, or white too cold. Here's a quick temperature tip: Red wine is served best at 50-55ºF; White wines can be as low as 45ºF; Rose should be somewhere in between. If you don't have good wine storage, simply remember the rule of 20. Remove white wine from the fridge 20 minutes before serving, and place red wine in the fridge 20 minutes before serving.

5 Ounces of Wine is a glass. Try pouring the wine in your favorite glass up to the level you normally enjoy. Then pour the wine in a measuring cup. Shocking, isn't it? To enjoy wine, pour your glass a third full. This allows all the aromas to release when you swirl and smell.

Compare and Contrast wines. Once a week open two or three bottles, and taste before indulging. It's fun to do this by grape varietal. What's the difference between a California Sauvignon Blanc and one from New Zealand? What flavors and aromas can you identify that make each wine unique? Is the color different? How about the wine's staying power – does the taste linger or does it immediately disappear?

Contradictions. Here's where I contradict myself. Even though you may normally enjoy affordable wine, make sure you splurge every once in a while and buy the best. Develop a relationship with a good wine shop and ask for advice on a wine with typicity. Typicity is "wine speak" for a wine with the color, the aroma, the taste and finish typical of the blend or the grape. This is a super way to know what a specific wine or grape variety should taste like.

Eating while drinking is an integral part of the wine experience. The taste of wine changes with the food we eat with it, and the changes are predictable based on certain factors. For instance, foods that are sweet make any wine taste stronger/bolder. In contrast, sour and salty food components make the wine taste milder and fruitier. There are other food and wine interactions that trick our palate, and make the world of food and wine pairing so interesting.

Bring the element of fun into your wine tasting. Go wild and crazy. Every once in a while, purchase a bottle with absolutely no forethought. Like the label? Buy it. The name makes you smile? Buy it. The color of the bottle matches your eyes? Buy it. Who knows when you will score a homerun?

Last but not least, **don't be afraid to try anything and express your opinion.** Remember that if you think a wine smells like grapes – you're right! Don't miss The Four Easy Steps to Taste Wine in the appendix.

Wine Words

Wine is an adventure that begins with the opening of a bottle - a captivating story of land, romance, science, history and intrigue. I hope you'll share my passion with me as you learn to enjoy the interplay of good food and wine

Wine is full of contradictions and it's never static. Each year brings a new harvest to try, fascinating innovations to unearth, and fundamental principles to discover again and again. The great news is: you don't have to be a wine guru to take pleasure in a glass, you can learn by simply by tasting and enjoying. Be forewarned though, once you catch the bug you may be hopelessly hooked!

The wine pairings with each recipe are designed to be informative and accessible. How frustrating to read mouth watering wine reviews only to discover distribution is limited to one state, the taster has been sent an exclusive bottle, or there were only 6 cases produced and the wine starts at 3 figures. I have solved that problem in the Friday Four. The wines chosen are widely available in familiar stores, and the approximate price paid has been noted.

Discover wine that you like, that is affordable to drink often. That's the Taste and Savor wine philosophy. Once you have tasted the wine pairing suggested, I hope you will have the confidence to decide on your own pairings. Whether traditional or innovative, with just a little knowledge you can discover your own palate and the excitement of uncovering your own perfect match. Let the tasting begin!

appetizers

Firsts, starters, tapas, meze, antipasti, finger food, I love them all!
Each bite bursting with flavor – a tasty hint of what's to come.
And what's better than a meal of grazing? Two or three delicious
small plates of colorful and interesting foods, each one with
its distinctive tastes, textures and flavors.

The recipes in this chapter are designed to whet the appetite
of your friends and family – a start to a delicious meal. But don't
forget you can increase the serving size and make it a main course
by simply adding a salad and good loaf of crusty bread. Prepare
2 or 3 ahead of time and pack them in a basket for tailgating,
picnics or concerts. Invite the team over and share the fun food
along with a new favorite bottle of wine. Mix, mingle
and munch with neighbors and friends. No matter how you
enjoy them, appetizers are the life of the party!

1

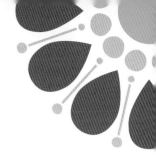

Artichokes and Peppers with Basil Balsamic Vinaigrette

This is a perfect make-ahead recipe for an appetizer, a potluck or a casual dinner with family and friends. Full of good-for-you fiber and nutrition, its beautiful colors make it the star of any table. Change it from appetizer to salad by serving it on a bed of shredded romaine lettuce - add a loaf of bread and a bottle of wine and you have dinner!

3 Boxes Frozen Artichoke Hearts, defrosted

1 TB Extra Virgin Olive Oil

1 Tsp each Sea Salt and Pepper

3 Red, Yellow or Orange Peppers, roasted and cut into Thin Strips

Basil-Balsamic Vinaigrette

¾ Cup (¼") Cubed Asiago, Fontina or other Semi Soft Italian Cheese

¼ Cup Capers, drained

¼ Cup Kalamata Olives, chopped

¼ Cup chopped Basil

Vegetarian

Artichokes and Peppers
with Basil Balsamic Vinaigrette

Step One
Toss the artichoke hearts, olive oil and salt and pepper together.
Place on a sheet pan and roast for 20 – 30 minutes at 400°F.

Step Two
Toss the peppers and roasted artichoke hearts with about half of the vinaigrette.
Place on a large platter and top with the cheese, capers, olives and basil.

Basil-Balsamic Vinaigrette

1 Garlic Clove, grated

2 TB Dry Red Wine

2 TB Balsamic Vinegar

1 Tsp Dijon Mustard

½ Cup Basil Leaves, (Packed)

¼ - ½ Cup Extra Virgin Olive Oil

Sea Salt and Black Pepper to taste

Place the first 5 ingredients in a food processor or blender and process well.
Drizzle in the olive oil, and season with salt and pepper.

 Taste and Savor TV: Roasting Peppers

Kitchen Smidgen
Fontina cheese is a classic Italian cheese made from cow's milk. With a 45% milk fat content, the cheese is creamy and rich with a nutty flavor, which gets stronger with aging. Not only is it good as a slicing cheese – but luscious and smooth when melted.

get creative

Asiago, pronounced ah-SYAH-goh, is a delicious mild cheese, named for the region in the Italian Alps where it was first produced. There are two types: pressato (fresh) and d'allevo (mature). The cheese, made with whole milk from grass fed cows is matured for 20 to 40 days. The fresh is smooth and creamy and the mature is crumbly and tangy.

Tasty Wine Tip

Michele Chiarlo Barbera d'Asti   *Piedmont, Italy*
Total Wine about $13.00

Did you know that there are over 350 grape varieties growing in Italy? One you shouldn't miss is Barbera (bar-BEH-ra). Barbera is a black (red) grape that has cherry flavors, soft tannins, and medium to high acidity. A perfect pick with almost any Italian meal - and easy on the wallet as well!

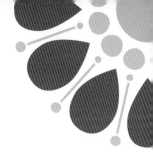

Creamy Pumpkin Peanut Soup

I love the word "unctuous" applied to food, don't you? It's the creamy, rich texture of sauces and soups, mousses and flourless cakes that keeps us coming back for one more little bite. This soup achieves that texture nirvana by pureeing the veggies and adding them back into the pot. And topping the soup? A hit of crunch and salt with a sprinkle of chopped roasted peanuts.

2 Cans (15 oz) Solid Pack Pumpkin

36 oz Low Fat/Salt Veggie Broth

12 oz Pear or Apricot Nectar

½ Cup Natural, Creamy Peanut Butter

1 TB grated Fresh Ginger

¼ Cup thinly Sliced Green Onions (Green Tops only)

1 Clove Garlic, grated

1 TB Fresh Lime Juice

1 TB Fresh Orange Juice

Pinch of Cayenne Pepper

Sea Salt and freshly cracked black pepper to taste

Zest of 1 Lime

½ Cup Greek Yogurt

¼ Cup finely chopped, Roasted Salted Peanuts

Vegetarian

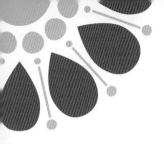

Creamy Pumpkin Peanut Soup

Step One
In a medium stockpot, combine the pumpkin, veggie broth, and pear or apricot nectar. Bring to a boil over high heat. Reduce the heat to low, and simmer for about 15 minutes.

Step Two
Remove 1 cup of the pumpkin mixture from the pot. In a blender or a food processor, process the pumpkin mixture with peanut butter until smooth. Return to the pot. Add the ginger, green onion, garlic, juices and cayenne pepper. Cook, stirring occasionally for 15 minutes over medium heat. Taste for salt and pepper.

Step Three
Mix the lime zest with the Greek yogurt. Garnish each bowl with a TB of the yogurt mixture, and sprinkle with the peanuts.

Taste and Savor TV: Toasting Nuts, Chopping Herbs

Kitchen Smidgen
The thickness of the juice is what makes "Nectar" different from other juices. Some fruits have juice that would be very thick to drink straight up, so they are diluted with water. Nectar does have a great deal of sugar in it though, so it is best used in recipes like this instead of drinking it straight up. If you like the taste, try cutting some of the extreme sweetness with sparkling water.

get creative

Solid Pack Pumpkin is just what it sounds like: 100% pure pumpkin with nothing else added. You can make your own pumpkin puree – but the canned version is delicious and saves you all the work of seeding, roasting, scooping and pureeing. When making your own – don't use a Halloween-type pumpkin. Look for a "pie" pumpkin with names like sugar, cheese or milk pumpkin. Any recipe that calls for pumpkin also works great with fresh butternut squash, or even sweet potatoes. To get your measurements correct with substitutions, a 15 oz can of pumpkin contains just a little less than 2 cups.

Tasty Wine Tip

Brancott Pinot Noir   *Marlborough, New Zealand*
Total Wine about $10.00

A perfect light red for the fall season, this Beaujolais is an earthy, strawberry, black pepper refresher that rises to the occasion with the pumpkin soup and would not be amiss sitting on the Thanksgiving table, or with any fall-spiced roasted chicken or pork.

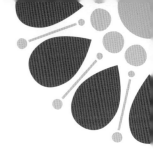

Cilantro
Shrimp

This dish is inspired by my love of crisp, clean and green cilantro - it's a great way to spice up a weeknight. Plus, all the ingredients are combined in the food processor, so not a lot of chopping. Add a green salad with vinaigrette made with lime juice, and a crusty baguette. Voila! You have dinner for family or friends.

The Shrimp
2 TB Extra Virgin Olive Oil
½ Cup Cilantro Stems and Leaves
4 Cloves peeled Garlic
1 Tsp Sea Salt
1 TB Ground White Pepper
2 TB Light Brown Sugar
2 TB Fish Sauce
1 LB Large Shrimp, peeled

The Dipping Sauce
¼ Cup Cilantro Stems and Leaves
2 Cloves peeled Garlic
1 Jalapeño Pepper, Seeds and Ribs
    removed
$\frac{1}{3}$ Cup Fresh Lime Juice
Zest of a Lime
2 TB Light Brown Sugar
2 TB Fish Sauce
Chopped Cilantro for garnish

Pescetarian

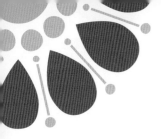

Cilantro Shrimp

The Shrimp
Step One
Put the oil, cilantro, garlic, salt, pepper, sugar and fish sauce in a food processor or blender. Mix to form a paste.

Step Two
Place the shrimp and the cilantro paste in a zippy bag. Place in the fridge for at least 1 hour - up to 3 hours.

Step Three
Remove the shrimp from the fridge, discard the marinade. Preheat a grill, grill pan or broiler on high. Cook the shrimp until just pink - about 2 minutes per side.

The Dipping Sauce
Place all the ingredients in the food processor or blender. Mix until well combined. Serve the shrimp with the Cilantro Dip, garnished with chopped cilantro.

 Taste and Savor TV: Grating Garlic and Ginger

Kitchen Smidgen
White Peppercorns start out the same as black peppercorns, but are allowed to ripen longer on the vine. The hard black shell is removed to produce a spice with a slightly hotter flavor than black peppercorns.

get creative

Fish Sauce is an essential ingredient in Thai and other Asian cuisines. Called "Nam Pla" in Thai, it is used liberally to marinate fish and meat, or mixed with chilies and lime juice for a dipping sauce. Thais use fish sauce as a condiment just like we use salt and pepper. Next time you want to add a little Asian flair to a dish - try fish sauce!

Tasty Wine Tip

Pine Ridge Chenin Blanc Viognier  *California*
Costco about $10.00

Savoring a glass of Pine Ridge with the limey-fresh taste of Cilantro Shrimp is a match made in heaven. The Chenin Blanc grape is native to France's Loire Valley - but is expressed perfectly in the tang of acidity, green apple and pear flavors of this wine. The Viognier contributes a plush mouth feel and some light floral notes.

Grilled Corn Salad Wraps

*It doesn't get better than this with fresh crunchy
summer corn on the cob. Perfect as a starter for
a backyard barbeque – it can also star on its on as a
delicious veggie dinner!*

Vegetarian

6 Ears of Corn
1 Red Bell Pepper
1 Red Onion, quartered
Olive Oil for Grilling Vegetables
1 Cup chopped Tomatoes
1 Ripe Avocado, chopped
4 oz Monterey Jack Cheese, in ¼
   inch cubes
¼ Cup chopped Cilantro
Butter or Bibb Lettuce
Warm Corn Tortillas
Crispy Tortilla Strips

The Dressing

¼ Cup Lime Juice
¼ Cup Extra Virgin Olive Oil
1 Tsp Freshly Ground Black Pepper
2 Tsp Sea Salt
2 Tsp Ground Cumin

Kitchen Smidgen

The easiest way to cut the corn off the cob is to stand it vertically
in a shallow bowl or baking dish. Using a sharp knife, make long
downward strokes as you move around the cob.

get creative

Crispy Tortilla Strips are a fun garnish for this salad - and lots of other dishes! Take 2 corn tortillas and cut them in to skinny strips - about ⅛ inch wide. In a small skillet, heat 1 TB of canola oil until very hot. Drop ½ of the strips into the oil and stir until lightly browned - they will cook quickly. Remove, salt lightly and cook the other half.

Step One
Preheat your grill for 10 minutes. Lightly oil the corn, pepper, and onion. Over medium heat, grill for about 5-7 minutes or until brown in spots. Place the pepper in a zippy bag and set aside.

Step Two
Make the dressing by combining all the ingredients in a jar and shaking it.

Step Three
Remove the pepper from the zippy bag, peel and chop. Cut the corn off the cob, and chop the red onion. Place in a bowl and add the tomatoes, avocado, cheese and cilantro. Toss with the salad dressing. Garnish with crispy tortilla strips. Serve with lettuce and tortillas.

 *Taste and Savor TV:*

Cutting and Roasting Peppers
Peeling and Chopping Avocados
Chopping and Seeding Tomatoes
Making Salad Dressing

Tasty Wine Tip
Santa Maria Sauvignon Blanc  *Casablanca Valley, Chile*
Total Wine about $16.00

The most successful matches with "South of the Border" tastes are fresh, sleek and crisp with acidity. And wine is no exception. The green herb and grapefruit flavors of Santa Maria Sauvignon Blanc pair with the rich avocado and smoky cumin perfectly - it's clean and light enough to pick up the taste of the spices and vegetables. Sit back, relax and enjoy a refreshing glass with your Grilled Corn Salad Wraps!

Grilled Scallops and Apples

This appetizer is a taste "party" in your mouth: a super combination of briny sweet seafood, crisp Granny Smith apples and smooth, luscious honey. Peppery basil gathers up all the flavors and gives them zip. Try this when crunchy apples are in season – or any time!

 *Pescetarian*

2 Granny Smith Apples, cored
12 Large Sea Scallops
2 TB Olive Oil
Sea Salt and Freshly Ground Black Pepper
2 TB Rice Vinegar
2 TB Honey
8 Basil Leaves, chopped
1 Lemon, thinly sliced

Kitchen Smidgen

Did you know the darker the honey - the better it is for you? Try seeking out Chestnut Honey for an explosion of deep, dark flavor.

get creative

If you haven't grilled fruit before – its time! Top grilled apples with a little honey and cinnamon when they are hot off the grill - and serve with a scoop of vanilla ice cream or frozen yogurt. Try grilling peaches or mango slices for knock-out salsa. Serve grilled pineapple slices with halved red grapes, a chopped mango and two TB Maple Syrup for a killer fruit salad!

Step One
Make sure your grill or grill pan is hot. Cut your apples into ¼ inch slices.

Step Two
Pat the scallops and the apples dry with a paper towel. Brush them with the olive oil. Grill the apple slices for about a minute a side, remove, and place 3 - 4 slices on each plate. Sprinkle the scallops with salt and pepper and grill for about 2-3 minutes per side. Place the scallops on the apple slices.

Step Three
Whisk the rice vinegar and honey together and drizzle over the apples. Garnish with basil and lemon slices.

Taste and Savor TV:
Chopping Herbs

Tasty Wine Tip

Clos Du Bois Chardonnay   *California*
Kroger about $10.00

Nothing else compliments the light texture of the scallops and the sweetness of the honey like a soft chardonnay. The Clos Du Bois has aromas of lime, pineapple, pear and the same green apple that you have grilled! It's medium body and citrus, pear and vanilla-caramel taste is a perfect foil for the honey and basil. This California white is barrel fermented to integrate oak and fruit flavor - the oak from the barrels produce the buttery vanilla-caramel flavor.

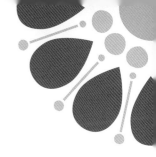

Jerk Chicken
Skewers

As a flight attendant in my twenties, I loved trips to the Caribbean. Jerk was my favorite food, and it didn't matter what it was on – fish, shellfish, chicken, pork, even goat! Nowadays, I have a wonderful friend from Barbados who is so generous with recipes and with treats when she returns from the island. She was the inspiration for this recipe! Try it as an appetizer, or a fun meal with family or friends. Plus, the jerk marinade is delicious on fish or pork, too.

4 Cloves Garlic
1 Large Yellow Onion, chopped
2 Habanero OR Jalapeños, seeded
1 Bunch Green Onions, chopped
1 TB Dried Thyme
1½ Tsp Ground Allspice
1" Piece Fresh Ginger
1 Tsp Each Salt and Black Pepper
¼ Cup Dark Rum
¼ Cup Molasses
4 Limes, zested and juiced

4 Large Boneless Skinless Chicken
   Breasts, in 1" Pieces
Prepared Fresh Fruit Skewers
Pomelo, Grapefruit or Pineapple to
   place the skewers

Flexitarian

Jerk Chicken Skewers

Step One

Place garlic, onion, chiles, green onions, thyme, allspice, ginger, salt and pepper
into a food processor; blend until smooth. Transfer the mixture to a large bowl,
and stir in rum, molasses, lime zest and juice. Place chicken in bowl, and turn to coat.
Marinate an hour.

Step Two

Remove the chicken from the marinade, and thread onto skewers. Boil the marinade
in a small saucepan for at least 5 minutes.

Step Three

Preheat the grill or a grill pan. Brush the grate or pan with oil, and slowly cook the
chicken until slightly charred and cooked through, brushing with the marinade when
you turn the meat. They will cook quickly: 5 - 6 minutes. Place the skewers in the large
fruit and serve with the fruit skewers.

Taste and Savor TV: Chopping Onions, Using Chiles

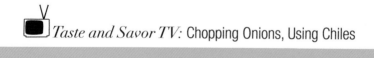

Kitchen Smidgen

Jerk is a style of cooking native to Jamaica in which meats or fish are dry-rubbed with
a tangy spice mixture. Three things are included in every jerk rub, chile peppers,
allspice and thyme, along with the cook's choice of onions, citrus, herbs and
other spices. To kick up the "heat" in this recipe, use habaneros or scotch
bonnet peppers. If you want the meat to be flavorful without the burn,
stick to the jalapeños.

get creative

The Pomelo is the largest member of the citrus fruit family and is grown and enjoyed all over the world in tropical climates. Delicious and juicy, it tastes like a grapefruit with out any bitterness.

Tasty Wine Tip
Indaba Chenin Blanc   Western Cape, South Africa,
Total Wine at about $9.00

This 100% Chenin Blanc is a crisp, crowd pleaser loaded with luscious tropical fruit, lime and floral aromas. These same fruit flavors follow through in the taste, with refreshing acidity and a slightly spicy finish. The African word Indaba derives from a Zulu term meaning "an assembly of the chiefs."

Rich Wild Mushroom Soup

I love soups that taste creamy and rich, don't you? Unfortunately they are often full of cream and butter – two ingredients not on my Top 10! So, when you try this soup you won't believe there is only 2 TB of cream in the whole recipe. Blending the soup with just a touch of cream for taste is the secret of the rich and silky texture.

 Vegetarian

2 TB Unsalted Butter, divided
1 TB Olive Oil
1 Yellow Onion, finely chopped
16 Oz White Mushrooms, chopped
1 Oz Dried Wild Mushrooms
6 Cups Light Veggie Stock
4 Cups Water

½ LB Wild Mushrooms, sliced
2 TB Parsley or Thyme
1 TB Fresh Lemon Juice
2 TB Heavy Cream
½ Cup Nonfat Greek Yogurt
Salt and Black Pepper to taste

Serve the Soup With:

Blue Cheese Toasts: 1 Small Baguette thinly sliced, Blue Cheese at Room Temperature, and Freshly Cracked Black Pepper

Toast the slices in a 350°F oven for about 5 minutes per side. Mash the blue cheese, top the toasts with the cheese and slide under the broiler until the cheese begins to melt. Remove and sprinkle with pepper.

Kitchen Smidgen

Most recipes call for you to soak dried mushrooms first. Since we are cooking them in with our chicken stock, no presoaking is required.

get creative

Because wild mushrooms are composed of mostly water, when they are dried the natural flavors are intensified - making them even more delicious. Even better, they have long storage life, up to a year, so you can enjoy their rich taste easily.

Step One
Melt 1 TB butter with the oil in a large stockpot over medium heat. Add the onion and cook until softened – about 7 minutes. Add the white mushrooms, dried mushrooms, stock and water and bring to a boil. Reduce the heat and simmer until the dried mushrooms are tender, about 30 minutes. Let cool slightly.

Step Two
While the soup is cooking, sauté the wild mushrooms in the remaining TB of butter until any liquid has evaporated. Add the herbs.

Step Three
Puree the soup in a blender until smooth. Place back into the stockpot, and add the sautéed wild mushrooms, lemon juice and cream. Simmer until warm, remove from the heat, stir in the yogurt and add salt and pepper to taste.

 *Taste and Savor TV:*
Chopping Onions

Tasty Wine Tip
A to Z Wineworks, Pinot Noir *Oregon*
Total Wine at about $18.00

The boast that A to Z Wineworks makes, "Aristocratic Wines at Democratic Prices", is true. You'll enjoy classic Pinot flavors, the taste of deeply concentrated red and black cherries with light tannins, and great balance. After trying A to Z, you'll agree that the traditional match of mushrooms and Pinot Noir is perfect with this wild mushroom soup.

Traditional Cheese Fondue

*The Swiss, originators of this creamy treat, serve their cheese
fondue in a glazed ceramic pot called a Caquelon. Regardless
of what kind of pot you own, break it out, dust it off, and join
me for a wonderful family or date night meal. Pour a glass of
Gruner Veltliner, hand out the Fondue Forks and
start dipping!*

 Vegetarian

½ LB Gruyere Cheese
½ LB Emmenthaler Cheese
2 TB Cornstarch
1 Garlic Clove
1 TB Lemon Juice
1 Cup Dry White Wine
1 TB Imported Kirschwasser

For Serving:
Baguette Cubes, Boiled Baby Potatoes and Barely Steamed Broccoli

Kitchen Smidgen

How to get rid of that garlic smell on your hands? Rub them on Stainless
Steel. Turn over a pan, or run your hands over the sides of your stainless
sink. Voila - No more stinky smell!

get creative

Kirshwasser is a type of liquor called an Eau de Vie. It's extremely high alcohol with a strong taste. A bottle of imported Kirshwasser is a must for this recipe. The best comes from Alsace in France - Trimbach is a brand that is available almost everywhere. Once you have your good bottle of this cherry goodness, try marinating some fresh berries in it for a luscious and easy dessert.

Step One

Shred the cheese coarsely, and place them in a zippy bag. Add the cornstarch and shake the bag to coat well. Set aside.

Step Two

Smash the garlic clove, remove the papery skin and rub the inside of your fondue pot with the garlic - then discard the clove. To your prepared pot, add the lemon juice and wine.

Step Three

Over medium heat, warm the wine mixture. Turn the heat to low and add the shredded cheese cooking and stirring constantly. Don't worry if it looks like it is separating - it will come together in the end. When the cheese is melted, add the 1 TB of Kirshwasser. (If children are joining you - just leave it out.) Serve the Fondue with Baguette Cubes, Boiled Baby Potatoes and Barely Steamed Broccoli.

Tasty Wine Tip

LOIS Gruner Veltliner 🍇 *Austria (Kamptal Region)*
Whole Foods about $15.00

Have you tried Gruner Veltliner? If you are a fan of Sauvignon Blanc, you will love it. One of the first things you should know is that Veltliner is pronounced "leaner" not liner. It's a zingy, refreshing white from Austria that is perfect with Cheese Fondue! It's crunchy green apple and grapefruit flavors cut through the richness of the cheese perfectly. It's fairly low alcohol, (12%) so you can have a glass without "taking to the couch".

Pat's Shrimp Cocktail

Zippy, fresh and cool, this shrimp cocktail is perfect for an appetizer, salad or a light dinner. My sister, Pat, inspired this flavorful recipe. She always adds a special touch to every dish - making it distinctive and delicious. So when I sat down to create a shrimp cocktail for a luncheon recently, I asked myself, "What would Pat do?" I hope you like my discovery!

 *Pescetarian*

1 TB grated Garlic
¼ Cup minced Shallots
¼ Cup Cilantro, chopped
2 TB Clamato Juice Cocktail
½ Cup Light Ketchup
2 – 4 TB Fresh Lime Juice
1 Tsp Chipotle Tabasco, or to taste
¼ Cup Horseradish
Sea Salt and Freshly Ground Pepper
  to taste
2 Ripe Avocados, peeled, pitted and
  in ½" Cubes
2 LBs Cooked Large or Extra Large
Shrimp, peeled and deveined
Shredded Romaine Lettuce
Lemon Wedges

Stir garlic, shallots, and cilantro together in a bowl. Add the Clamato, ketchup, lime juice, chipotle pepper sauce, and horseradish. Season with salt and pepper. Gently stir in avocado. Cover, and refrigerate 2 to 3 hours. Serve the shrimp on a bed of shredded lettuce topped with the cocktail sauce and a lemon wedge.

Taste and Savor TV:
Peeling and Chopping Avocados
Grating Garlic and Ginger
Chopping Herbs

Kitchen Smidgen

The first rule for cooking shrimp: Don't Overcook. First, shell and devein the shrimp. For each pound of shrimp, use 4-6 cups of water. You don't need a lot of seasoning - salt works great. Just like your pasta water, your shrimp water should taste like the sea. Bring the water to a rolling bowl and add in the shrimp. As soon as they are all pink – take them out and pour them in a colander. Done. Perfect, tender shrimp.

get creative

Clamato is a clam juice and tomato juice combo. It's a great addition to cocktail sauce, but also makes a super stock for a fish stew or Manhattan Clam Chowder. Or, if you are so inclined, a delicious Bloody Mary. Find it in the juice aisle at the grocery store.

Tasty Wine Tip

Château du Jaunay Muscadet de Sèvre-Et-Maine Sur Lie
Loire Valley, France   Total Wine about $11.00

Crisp, refreshing, lemon and lime are great descriptors for this delicious white. Melon de Bourgogne is the grape used in the wine, grown almost exclusively in the Loire Valley of France. It's made with the "Sur Lie" process, which means it has been aged on the yeast cells of the grapes, giving it good complexity. A super bargain for its traditional accompaniment, shellfish, once you try it you'll be hooked!

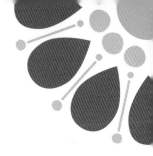

Thai Coconut
Shrimp Soup

This recipe always reminds me of the laughter of friends. The first time I prepared this for my friend Sara, she asked me why I had bought "Light" coconut milk. I replied that I wanted to save fat and calories in the soup. "Look at the ingredients, Nancy" she said. I did. That's when I learned that "Light" coconut milk is simply coconut milk and water. We laughed together and I haven't bought it since. Coconut milk keeps great in the freezer, so measure half of what you need in your recipe, add water as the other half, and store the rest in a zippy bag in the freezer.

1 TB Canola Oil

2 TB Fresh Ginger, grated

3 Cloves Garlic, grated

1 Tsp Chili Garlic Sauce, or more to taste, (in the international section of your grocery store)

½ Tsp Cracked Black Pepper

1½ Tsp Cumin

4 Cups Veggie Broth

1 Pkg Chinese Noodles (Mein) or Angel Hair Pasta

1 Cup Julienned Carrots

1½ Cups Light Coconut Milk

½ Pound Medium Shrimp, peeled

1 TB Fresh Lime Juice

2 TB chopped Cilantro

3 TB sliced Green Onions

Pescetarian

Thai Coconut Shrimp Soup

Step One

In a stockpot, heat the oil over medium high heat. Add the garlic, ginger, chili garlic sauce, pepper and cumin. Stir fry for about 1 minute to release the flavors. Add the broth and simmer for 10 minutes.

Step Two

Add the noodles and carrots to the broth and simmer for 1 minute. Add the coconut milk and simmer for 5 minutes.

Step Three

Add the shrimp, lime juice and cilantro. Cook until the shrimp are just pink about 2-3 minutes. Taste for seasoning - add a little more chili garlic sauce if necessary. Serve garnished with the sliced green onions.

Taste and Savor TV: Grating Garlic and Ginger, Chopping Herbs

Kitchen Smidgen

Chinese Noodles (Mein) The noodles used in Lo Mein or Chow Mein are made of wheat, so thin angel hair pasta can be substituted. For a change, use rice noodles: simply soak them in hot water for 5 minutes before adding them to the soup at the last minute.

get creative

Chili Garlic Sauce is an international ingredient that deserves a place in your pantry. I like the "Sriracha" brand. When you combine it with ketchup it makes a zingy dip for boiled shrimp or baked fries. Add it to a little mayo and you have a great spread for a sandwich. There's no limit to the fun you can have with this tangy, flavor filled condiment!

Tasty Wine Tip

Michel Leon Gewurztraminer  *Alsace, France*
Trader Joe's about $8.00

Rich golden color, honey and apricots and a full mouth feel make this a perfect pairing for the slightly spicy shrimp soup. You'll be drinking Gewurtz from its homeland - Alsace still grows the most of this spicy, aromatic grape. You can also find some good examples from California, Oregon and Washington State.

breakfast and brunch

It sounds cliché to say it, but breakfast is my favorite meal of the day.
Add friends and a late wake up, call it brunch and my day is perfect. Here's a
collection of a few of my favorite easy, quick and delicious morning recipes.
Add a bowl of fruit; some fresh hot coffee or a steaming kettle of tea and
breakfast is ready. Even if you don't bound out of bed ready for the day, these
dishes will make the morning easy to handle, and taste great!

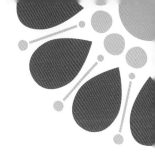

Shrimp and Grits

This is my hands down favorite Brunch dish. I've always been a shrimp and grits fan, but didn't order or make it because it is so full of fat and calories. I knew that there had to be a secret to making luscious grits without all the butter and cream. I discovered the secret in Greenville, South Carolina. The chef used cream cheese to make the grits unctuous and rich. I brought the idea home and played around – and discovered that just a quarter cup of soft light cream cheese and some shredded Parmesan make the perfect velvety bed for the spicy shrimp!

The Grits
1½ cups Stone-ground Grits, NOT Instant
1 Tsp Sea Salt
¼ Cup Soft Low Fat Cream Cheese
½ Cup shredded Parmesan
Bottle of Hot Pepper Sauce

Step One
Bring 6 cups of water and 1 Tsp salt to a boil. Whisk in the grits, reduce the heat to a simmer and cook over low heat for about 35 minutes, stirring often.

Step Two
When the grits are creamy, remove from the heat, and blend in the cream cheese and the Parmesan. Top the grits with the shrimp and gravy. (Recipe on following page.) Serve sprinkled with the bacon and accompanied by Hot Pepper Sauce.

Flexitarian

Shrimp and Grits

The Shrimp and Gravy

1LB Large Shrimp, peeled, deveined and halved lengthwise
Juice of 1 lemon
1 Tsp Sea Salt
½ Tsp Cayenne Pepper
3 Slices Turkey Bacon, finely chopped
½ Cup minced Red Onion
½ Cup minced Red Bell Pepper
6 Scallions, chopped
1 Garlic Clove, grated
2 TB Wondra or All-Purpose Flour
1 cup Low Fat/Salt Chicken Stock
Sea Salt and Black Pepper

Step One

Toss the shrimp with the juice, salt and cayenne. Set aside.

Step Two

Fry the bacon in a skillet over until crispy. Remove and set aside. Add the onion, and pepper, sauté until wilted, about 5 minutes. Add the scallions and garlic; sprinkle the flour over the mixture, sauté for 2 minutes. Stir in the stock and cook for 5 minutes. Add the shrimp to the gravy, sauté until just pink and season with salt and pepper.

 Taste and Savor TV: Chopping Onions, Grating Garlic and Ginger

Kitchen Smidgen

Stone-Ground Grits are just what they sound like – corn that is ground using millstones, often powered by a waterwheel. Quite coarsely ground, they have a rich taste and a thick and creamy texture. Because they are less processed than instant or quick grits, always store them in the fridge or freezer.

get creative

Wondra flour is quick mixing flour that dissolves quickly in liquid, making it the perfect choice for any stove top sauce. The other good news is that it's an all purpose flour with no additives. Grab a canister in your grocery store for easy smooth sauces and gravies.

Tasty Wine Tip

Ironstone Obsession Symphony   Sierra Foothills California
Cost Plus World Market, Total Wine about $8

Shrimp and grits – perfect any time of the day! And so is the wine for this week - lightly sweet, slightly fizzy and perfect to drink on its own or with a splash of fresh fruit juice. The grape used in this charmer is a cross between Muscat and Grenache Gris that thrives in the mineral-rich soils of California.

Baked Maple and Cinnamon French Toast

This is the recipe my house guests request over and over again for breakfast. I love it because its so quick, easy and delicious. On nights when I know a hectic morning is ahead, I prepare the dish all the way until baking and put it in the fridge. The next morning I pop in the oven for about 30 minutes and mix the syrup together. Almost instant breakfast! The smell wafts throughout the house enticing everyone down to the table.

 *Flexitarian*

6 (1 Inch-thick) Slices of Whole Wheat Bread
4 Eggs (or the equivalent egg substitute)
2 Cups Low Fat Milk (2%)
½ Cup Pure Maple Syrup
2 teaspoons Pure Vanilla Extract
½ Teaspoon Ground Cinnamon

Kitchen Smidgen

You can slide a pan of bacon into your oven at the same time as your French Toast. Place a rack inside a baking sheet and place your bacon slices on the rack, without having them touch. Cook for 5 to 10 minutes depending on desired doneness.

get creative

*And try using White Whole Wheat Flour in your holiday
recipes. You can add up to a third of the all-purpose flour
called for in your recipe. Your baked goods will taste just
as wonderful - and you will have added increased fiber,
vitamins and minerals.*

Step One
Preheat your Oven to 425°F. Spray a large baking pan or dish with non-stick butter spray. Arrange
the bread slices in a single layer. (The bread should fit into the pan, side by side, snugly.)

Step Two
In a medium sized bowl, combine the eggs, milk, maple syrup, vanilla and ground cinnamon. Beat
to blend and then pour over the bread. Let soak until all the egg mixture is absorbed, turning the
bread after about 10 minutes. Bake in your preheated oven for 15 minutes, then flip the bread and
bake for about 10 more minutes or until golden brown. Serve with Maple Cinnamon Syrup.

Maple Cinnamon Syrup:
1 Cup Pure Maple Syrup
½ Tsp Ground Cinnamon

Combine Maple Syrup and Ground Cinnamon in a heavy, small saucepan. Bring the syrup to a
Simmer. Remove from the heat, place the Baked French Toast on heated plates, top with the Warm
Maple Cinnamon Syrup and serve.

Tasty Wine Tip
Gluhwien, A German Mulled Wine, Bursting with Flavor!

My favorite Mulled Wine recipe. It's perfect for warming up holidays or any weekend breakfast
or brunch. Start with 2 bottles of Merlot or Pinot Noir. Pour the wine into a large pot on the
stove, and begin heating on very low heat. Add ½ Cup Sugar and stir. (As the wine gets warm
it will dissolve). Add 3 Cinnamon Sticks, 6 Whole Cloves, $1/8$ Tsp each Allspice and Mace. Pour
in ½ Cup Brandy, and add a thinly sliced Orange and Lemon. Steep for about an hour over low
heat - don't let it simmer at all - just keep the heat low and slow. Serve warm garnished with
more orange slices.

Perfect Pancakes

*Here is the recipe for the most scrumptious pancakes in the world.
Okay, I am a little biased. But I think you will have to agree when
you try them. Not only are they light, fluffy and delicious, they have
no added fat – so they are also low calorie. Plus, since they are
made with white beans, you are also getting your veggies.
Great way to give your kids their veggies, too!*

 *Vegetarian*

1 Cup Canned Cannellini Beans, drained and
   rinsed well
½ Cup Regular Oats
2 Eggs, room temperature
⅓ Cup Honey
½ Cup Skim Milk
½ Cup Whole Wheat Flour
1½ Tsp Baking Powder
½ Tsp Baking Soda
¼ Tsp Sea Salt

Kitchen Smidgen

Room Temperature Eggs are important when baking. They allow the fat in
the egg to incorporate more easily into the batter. To take eggs from
the fridge to room temp quickly, place them in a bowl of warm
water on the countertop for about 15 minutes before using.

get creative

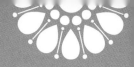

Good News! You can make these pancakes ahead of time - They hold great in the fridge. Just prepare, and let cool completely. Wrap in aluminum foil and place in the fridge. When ready to serve, pop in a 350°F oven for about 20 minutes to warm.

Step One
In a blender or food processor, combine the oatmeal and beans. Process until combined. Add the eggs, honey and milk and process again until well blended.

Step Two
In another bowl, toss together the flour, baking powder, baking soda and salt. Add the bean mixture and stir with a fork until just blended - a few lumps are fine.

Step Three
Drop the batter by ¼ cup full onto a skillet preheated on medium high heat. Cook for about 2 minutes for the first side. It will be ready to flip when the edges are set, and bubbles appear. Turn and cook the second side for about 1 minute. When done, Perfect Pancakes may be "browner" in color than other pancakes. Serve with your choice of syrup or honey.

Cheddar
Cheese Scones

Do you like scones as much as I do? If I am going to splurge,
I order a scone with my latte. The chubby sweet is always good,
but full of fat and calories. Here's an alternative. Made with
whole-wheat flour and just a little butter, this scone is a double
whammy: Easy AND indulgent. Try serving it warm from the
oven with a just a drizzle of honey - it's heaven.

Vegetarian

1½ Cups Whole Wheat Pastry Flour
½ Cup All Purpose Flour
2 Tsp Baking Powder
½ Tsp Baking Soda
½ Tsp Sea Salt
1 TB Sugar
3 TB Cold Unsalted Butter
1 Cup shredded Light Cheddar
⅓ Cup toasted chopped Pecans
¾ Cup Light Buttermilk
1 Large Egg, Beaten

Kitchen Smidgen

One of my favorite cooking teachers would say: "Remember, the crumblier
the dough is raw, the flakier it'll be baked". When you are working
biscuit, scone, tart or pastry dough handle it as little as possible.
Little gobs of butter in the formed dough are good!

get creative

If you don't have a Silpat non-stick baking mat, it's time to buy one. A Silpat will allow you to make baked goods, candy or even roast vegetables without sticking. No nonstick spray or parchment paper needed and the clean up is a breeze. Just a little soap and water and it's ready to put away. It's also great for rolling or patting out any kind of dough.

Step One
Preheat the oven to 400°F. Line a baking sheet with a Silpat or parchment paper.

Step Two
In a medium bowl, whisk together the flours, baking powder, baking soda, salt and sugar.

Step Three
Cut the butter into small pieces and add it to the flour mixture. Incorporate it with a pastry blender or knives until the mixture resembles coarse crumbs. Add the cheese, pecans, then buttermilk and stir until the dough comes together.

Step Four
Turn out the sticky, crumbly dough onto a piece of parchment or a Silpat. Gather the dough into a circle, approximately 8 inches across and 1 inch thick, being careful not to overwork the dough.

Step Five
Transfer the dough to the prepared baking sheet. Cut into 8 wedges and brush the tops with the egg. Pull the wedges apart to separate slightly. Bake for 20 minutes, or until lightly browned.

Tasty Wine Tip
S. Orsola Il Cortigiano Prosecco *Italy*
Total Wine about $10.00

Prosecco is Italy's popular answer to Champagne. This sparkler is just what you want for brunch - crisp, fresh flavors complemented by lots of tiny bubbles. It's off dry and full of peach and melon flavors. Try it with your scones and honey, accompanied by some cool fresh fruit.

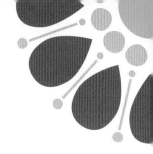

Strawberry Almond Waffles

I grew up eating waffles; both my mother and my sister make delicious ones. I remember when my sister lived in Tampa, Florida and I would spend summers with her. She made the most breathtakingly rich and indulgent coconut waffles – perfect for the tropical climate, (not so perfect for my figure!) My mother has always used the "Oh Boy" waffle recipe from the 1940s edition of the Better Homes and Gardens cookbook. Now that my dad is gone, she makes a batch and puts them in the freezer so that she can enjoy them often without trouble. That's what I'd like to encourage you to do as well. This recipe incorporates good-for-you ingredients in a quick batter that makes lots of waffles. This means that you will have a few to tuck in the freezer to enjoy later.

12-15 Whole Strawberries, sliced

¼ Cup Fresh Orange Juice

1¼ Cups All Purpose Flour

¾ Cup Whole Wheat Flour

1 TB Baking Powder

½ Tsp Salt

½ Cup toasted finely chopped Almonds

2 TB Fresh Orange Juice

1 TB Orange Zest

1¾ Cup Skim Milk

6 TB Canola or Vegetable Oil

2 Large Eggs

½ Cup Pureed Strawberries

Vegetarian

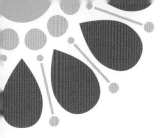

Strawberry Almond Waffles

Step One
To prepare the topping, toss the sliced strawberries and the ¼ cup orange juice together in a bowl - set aside.

Step Two
Combine the flours, baking powder, salt in a bowl and whisk well. Add the chopped almonds.

Step Three
In another bowl, stir together the 2 TB orange juice, zest, skim milk, oil, eggs and strawberries together.

Step Four
Fold the wet ingredients into the dry ingredients. Let stand for 10 minutes.

Step Five
Preheat your waffle iron. When hot, use a scant ½ cup batter for each waffle. Remove when golden brown and serve with the prepared strawberry topping.

Kitchen Smidgen

When you are using baking powder in a recipe, make sure you incorporate it well with the other dry ingredients. This can be done by sifting the ingredients together or by whisking in the powder.

get creative

Citrus zest can add lots of flavor without adding additional liquid to your recipes. Here's how to figure out how many lemons, limes or oranges you need to zest for your recipe: Medium lemon or lime - 1 TB of zest, Medium orange - 2 TB of zest. Try using zest in other baked goods - it will give them a "citrus lift"

Tasty Wine Tip

Greg Norman Sparkling Chardonnay/Pinot Noir  *Australia*
Total Wine about $16.00

Greg Norman can do more than play golf – his delicious wine from down under is perfect for brunch. Medium bodied with a rich long finish, you'll smell a hint of strawberry and citrus in this sparkler, and taste peaches and apricots with just a bit of lemon. It's made with the traditional sparkling wine grapes, Chardonnay and Pinot Noir, and is a perfect foil for the fruity goodness of the strawberry waffles.

Buttermilk Honey
Breakfast Cake

*How about an easy and delicious breakfast cake for a change? This is a great
morning treat to tuck in the kids lunch boxes, your sweetie's briefcase or even
your purse. I top this with strawberries in the recipe, but it's equally as delicious
with any kind of berries or fruit. When pineapples are on sale, I often chop one
and let it sit for 15 or 30 minutes until it becomes juicy – it creates its own sauce.
Perfect with a cup of tea or coffee, or even with a glass of the bubbly from the
Tasty Wine Tip. Wine with a special occasion brunch? Mais Oui!*

Vegetarian

1 Cup Flour
½ Cup Whole Wheat Flour
1 Tsp Baking Powder
1 Tsp Baking Soda
½ Tsp Ground Cinnamon
½ Tsp Ground Ginger
¼ Tsp Ground Cardamom
¼ Tsp Ground Nutmeg
½ Tsp Sea Salt
2 Egg Whites + 1 Large Egg
⅔ Cup Light Buttermilk
¾ Cup Honey, divided
⅓ Cup Vegetable or Canola Oil
1 TB Molasses
24 Large Strawberries, sliced
Vanilla Nonfat Yogurt

Kitchen Smidgen

Make sure to spray your measuring cup with nonstick spray when
measuring sticky ingredients like honey - it will slide right out with
little mess and easy clean up!

get creative

When a recipe calls for an ingredient, followed by the word "divided", it means that you will be using the ingredient in the recipe more than one time. For instance, in this recipe we used ½ cup of the honey in Step Three, and the remainder in Step Five.

Step One
Preheat the oven to 350°F. Spray a 9" square pan with nonstick spray.

Step Two
Whisk the flours, baking powder, baking soda, spices and salt together in a large bowl.

Step Three
In another bowl, whisk the eggs, buttermilk, and ½ cup of the honey, oil and molasses together.

Step Four
Make a well in the dry mixture and stir in the egg mixture, just until smooth. Pour the batter into the prepared pan and bake for 30 minutes, or until a toothpick inserted in the middle of the cake comes out with just a few crumbs.

Step Five
While the cake is cooking, toss the strawberries together with the remaining ¼ cup honey. When the cake is cool, cut in 12 squares and serve topped with the vanilla yogurt and the honey-macerated strawberries.

Tasty Wine Tip
Arthur Metz Cremant d'Alsace  *Alsace, France*
Total Wine about $15.00

Wine with breakfast definitely calls for a bright sparkler! It was only about 100 years ago that the "champagne method" of making wine was applied to the grapes of Alsace, creating Crémant d'Alsace. Made with mostly Pinot Blanc or Pinot Noir grapes, the resulting fizzy is light and crisp with hints of peaches and apricots. A great alternative to a traditional French champagne, and much less expensive as well.

☀ main dishes

Healthy, delicious, fast and flavorful, the recipes in this chapter are the centerpieces of any meal! You may have changed the way you think of main dishes over the past couple of years. Me, too! Before, I would have thought, "Okay, I have some chicken – what do I want to serve with it?" Now I find myself looking for alternatives. As a Flexitarian, (I eat 20% or less of my meals with meat or chicken), I enjoy the adventure of all foods and try to use ingredients in unique ways. Along with shifting your focus from meat based meals there are many ways to make mains healthier and delicious. Did you know that most of us don't take advantage of the wealth of herbs and spices available, except for a handful like parsley, sage, basil, rosemary and thyme?

Just by adding more flavors to your meals you can kick-start a new and better way of eating. Bringing the Mediterranean, India or Italy to our kitchens through cooking. How fun is that?

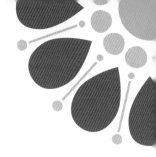

Chicken with Creamy
Wild Mushrooms

*I love recipes that fool the tongue with creamy goodness.
Who doesn't love a chicken, mushroom and cream dish? But
don't break out the heavy cream carton – or that red can.
You don't need to when you make this recipe; the cream
comes from the blender. Once you learn the technique of
pureeing veggies to create a creamy texture, you'll use the
trick again and again. And if you want to add that heavy
cream taste to a dish, puree and then add just 2 TB of
cream. All the lusciousness of heavy cream without lots of it.*

1½ Cups Light Chicken Stock
1 OZ Dried Mushrooms
2 TB Extra Virgin Olive Oil
1 Tsp Turmeric
½ Tsp Freshly Cracked Black Pepper
4 Chicken Breasts, Cut in half horizontally
1 Large Yellow Onion, chopped
12 OZ Mixed Wild Mushrooms, sliced
1½ Cups Nonfat Plain Greek Yogurt
Sea Salt to taste
2 Cups Cooked Brown Basmati Rice
Fresh Thyme for garnish

Flexitarian

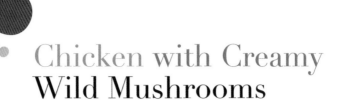

Chicken with Creamy
Wild Mushrooms

Step One

Preheat the oven to 300°F. Bring the stock to a boil in a medium saucepan. Add the dried mushrooms and simmer until the stock is reduced by half. Set aside in another pan. While the stock and mushrooms are simmering, warm the olive oil over medium heat. Add the turmeric and black pepper. Cook and stir for a minute until fragrant.

Step Two

Sauté the chicken breasts in the spice mixture. When browned on both sides, remove from the sauté pan and place in a 300°F oven for 3 -5 minutes to finish cooking. Remove from the oven and keep warm with aluminum foil.

Step Three

Add the onions and sauté over medium heat until wilted and golden. Add the fresh wild mushrooms and cook until mushrooms are soft.

Step Four

Remove half the fresh mushrooms and onions from the pan and add them to a blender. Add the stock with the dried mushrooms. Puree until smooth, add the yogurt and blend again. Add back to the pan with the remaining mushrooms and onions. Taste for salt

Step Five

Place the chicken on the rice, top with the mushroom sauce. Garnish with fresh thyme.

Taste and Savor TV: Chopping Onions, Cutting Chicken Breasts

Kitchen Smidgen

When using fresh thyme, you don't always have to strip the leaves from the stem. If you have thyme with soft tender stems like the picture above, you can just chop it - stem and all.

get creative

Next time you want to make a cream sauce, don't open the carton of heavy cream. Place some of your veggies in the blender - and then add them back to the sauce. You'll find the same creamy texture without all the fat!

Tasty Wine Tip

Hahn Estates Pinot Noir   *Monterey, California*
Kroger, Publix about $12.00

You've seen the rooster in the wine aisle - Nicky Hahn is the winemaker and Hahn means "rooster' in German. You'll enjoy dark fruit and floral aromas and a spicy taste of blackberries and chocolate. A great buy for delicious Pinot Noir from California!

Lemon Chicken Sliders
with Raisin Chutney

Here's the perfect entrée when you're in the picnic, party and potluck mood, Easy, lemony and fast, this recipe will please family and friends no matter where it's eaten. Plus, the chutney is terrific – so all you "jammers" out there please note – this is a super spread, pour or treat to put up!

Flexitarian

2 Lemons
8 Cups Raisins
1½ Cup Sugar
4 Cups Red Wine
⅓ Cup Balsamic Vinegar
1½ Tsp Ground Cloves
1 TB Sea Salt
1½ Tsp Ground Black Pepper
½ Cup Light Mayo
8 Cooked Chicken Thighs, preferably
  cooked with Garam Masala
12 Whole Wheat Dinner Rolls

Step One
Very thinly slice the lemons. (A mandoline or the slicing blade of a food processor is best for this job) Set aside for at least 2 hours.

Step Two
In the bowl of a food processor, add the raisins and sugar. Pulse to coarsely chop and place in a sauce pan along with the wine, vinegar, cloves, salt and pepper. Bring to a boil and then reduce to a simmer and cook and stir until syrupy – about 10 minutes, Remove from the heat and set aside to cool. (You can prepare ahead of time and place it in the fridge.)

Step Three
Roughly chop the sliced lemons and stir into the mayo. Chop the chicken. On the bottom of each roll layer the jam, then the chicken. Spread the top bun with the lemon mayo and place on the sandwich.

Taste and Savor TV: Using a Mandoline

Kitchen Smidgen

Cloves are flower buds that are dried and sold whole or dried. They have a distinctive, sweet flavor that many people recognize as an aroma of the holidays. They are native to Indonesia, and today are harvested mainly there, Sri Lanka, and India. The word is derived from the French word clou, meaning, "nail." No ground cloves in the cupboard? A good substitute for cloves is allspice.

get creative

This recipe makes LOTS of raisin chutney - on purpose! The chutney is wonderful over goat cheese, as a glaze for a pork tenderloin or even a topping for a cream-cheese-spread bagel. I usually share when I make it and it's a terrific hostess gift.

Tasty Wine Tip
Black Swan Shiraz SE Australia
Kroger, Publix about $8.00

You may have passed over this wine in the grocery store, but no more! A perfect wine to use when making the raisin chutney and enjoy with the sliders. Australian Shiraz is one of the best values in the market today especially those wines with the designation of South East (SE) Australia. Black Cherry plus spices and dark cocoa on the nose opens up to juicy jammy dark fruits on the taste.

Greek Lemon Chicken

*This chicken dish is one of my easiest "go to" weeknight dinner ideas.
Do a little sautéing, plop it all in a casserole dish, and it's done. Cook
up a quick side of brown rice or whole wheat orzo, steam a little
broccoli and you will have a tasty lemony-cheesy dinner that you and
your family will love. And the leftovers are just wonderful, tucked in a
pita and dolloped with Tzatziki sauce.*

 *Flexitarian*

1 TB Olive Oil
8 Boneless, Skinless Chicken Breasts
½ Cup diced Yellow Onion
2 Garlic Cloves, grated
½ Cup Fresh Lemon Juice

Zest of 1 Lemon
2 TB Dried Oregano Leaves
6 Ounces Feta Cheese, crumbled
½ Cup chopped Green Onions
Sea Salt and Black Pepper
Chopped Fresh Oregano

Step One
Heat the oil in a large skillet. Over medium high heat sauté the chicken breasts until browned,
or about 10 minutes. Remove and set aside. Sauté the onions until translucent and soft, about 5
minutes. Add the garlic and sauté for 1 minute.

Step Two
Turn the oven to 350°F. Place the chicken breasts in a "13x9x2" (or similar) casserole dish and spoon
the onions and garlic, the lemon juice, zest, dried oregano, feta and green onions over the chicken.
Sprinkle well with Sea Salt and black pepper.

Step Three
Bake for 45 minutes or until the chicken is done. Remove, garnish with fresh oregano and lemon
wedges. Serve with whole wheat orzo or brown rice.

 Taste and Savor TV: Cutting Chicken, Chopping Herbs

Kitchen Smidgen

Oregano is an aromatic herb native to Europe, the Mediterranean and Asia.
It's essential in Italian and Greek food and pairs well with mint, thyme
and parsley. Dried oregano is often more pungent than fresh!

get creative

Send leftover Greek Lemon Chicken to work or school tomorrow. Place the Chicken in Pita Pockets with Tzatiki Sauce - a delicious Greek yogurt sauce.

Peel, seed and finely chop 1 cucumber. Combine the cucumber with 1 cup non-fat yogurt, add 1 Tsp salt, 1 clove finely chopped garlic and 2 TB chopped fresh dill.

Tasty Wine Tip
Boutari Santorini White  *Santorini, Greece*
Total Wine about $17.00

If you're eating Greek food, why not try Greek wine? Santorini is not only the most famous and beautiful of Greek Islands, but the home to Santorini wine. The distinctive Assyrtiko grape brings fresh, dry, crisp and citrusy flavors to this light quaffer. You'll enjoy this food friendly choice with almost any chicken or fish dish.

Chicken
Satay Pitas

I read an article the other day about the amazing rise in popularity of Thai food. With its delicious, fresh ingredients and vibrant tastes, it doesn't surprise me! Does your family like Thai food? We certainly do. Here's an easy take on Chicken Satay that everyone will enjoy. A little like burgers, a lot like Satay with crisp and crunchy "peanutty" vegetables too!

 *Flexitarian*

⅓ Cup Natural Peanut Butter
2 TB Rice Vinegar
1 TB Soy Sauce
1 TB Sesame Oil
1 Tsp grated Fresh Ginger
2 TB Sweet Chili Sauce
Sea Salt and Black Pepper
1½ LB Ground Chicken
⅓ Cup minced Red Onion
⅓ Cup chopped Cilantro
3 TB Sweet Chili Sauce
½ Tsp each Sea Salt and Pepper
3 Cups shredded Napa Cabbage
1 Cup shredded Carrots
¼ Cup chopped Green Onions
6 Whole Wheat Pita Pockets

Kitchen Smidgen

Asian Sweet Chili Sauce is a sweet and mildly spicy Thai condiment readily available in the international section of your grocery store. Try it as a dipping sauce for chicken tenders or kebabs, too.

get creative

Rice Vinegar is a great substitute for other types of vinegar when you are serving wine with a salad. Some vinegars can be too strong – Rice Vinegar has less acidity and a pleasant light taste that will allow other ingredients, and also wine to shine!

Step One

To make the dressing, mix the first 6 ingredients together in a bowl. Taste for salt and pepper. Set aside. Mix the chicken, onion, cilantro, chili sauce and salt and pepper in another bowl; make 6 (one-inch) thick patties.

Step Two

On an oiled grill, (or grill pan), cook the burgers 7 to 8 minutes, turning once halfway, or until no longer pink in the center.

Step Three

Toss the dressing with the shredded cabbage, carrot and green onion. Split the pitas in half. Place some of the tossed salad in the pitas, and slide in the grilled chicken patties.

Taste and Savor TV:
Grating Garlic and Ginger

Tasty Wine Tip

Hogue Chenin Blanc 🍇 *Columbia Valley, Washington State*
Total Wine, Publix about $9.00

Crisp, refreshing, lemon zest and green apples are all words used to describe this "good buy" chenin blanc from Washington state. Chenin Blanc grapes are grown in France, (where the wine is called Vouvray), all the way to South Africa, (where it is called Steen), but wherever they grow, you can call it good. Well balanced in acidity and sweetness, you'll find this delicious wine a welcome change from the same old whites.

Thai Turkey Sliders

There are so many fun new burger restaurants opening all over the country. And not just the traditional beef on a bun – there is chicken, pork, lamb, bison, seafood, veggie – even delicious venison burgers. So, inspired by their diverse choices, I decided to expand my burger menu at home. My husband Mike, who is NOT a big burger fan, loves these sliders. They are a delicious and healthier twist on the ole standby, and so colorful with the carrots and cilantro. Try making a double batch of the BBQ sauce and basting chicken breasts with it on the grill. Delicious!

 *Flexitarian*

1 LB Ground Turkey	½ Tsp each Sea Salt and Pepper
2 TB Low-Sodium Soy Sauce	6 – 8 Whole Wheat Dinner Rolls
2 TB Hoisin Sauce	2 Cups shredded Napa Cabbage
1 Clove of Garlic, grated	Ginger Lime BBQ Sauce
1 shredded Carrot	Fresh Jalapeño Slices (if desired)
2 TB chopped Cilantro	

Step One
In a medium bowl, combine the first 8 ingredients. Using your hands, mix to distribute the seasonings evenly throughout the meat. Form 6 to 8 half-inch thick sliders. (They will be very moist.)

Step Two
Make sure your grill is clean and oiled. Preheat the grill, or a grillpan on high. Cook the burgers for about 5 minutes per side. Remove and set aside. Split and spray the dinner rolls with Pam, (or brush with oil). Place on the grill for 1-2 minutes or until crusty and brown.

Step Three
Toss the napa cabbage with the BBQ Sauce. Assemble the sliders by placing the meat on the bun, and top with the napa cabbage and jalapeños.

 Taste and Savor TV: Grating Garlic and Ginger, Chopping Herbs

Kitchen Smidgen

Hailing from China, tall and thin Napa Cabbage is slightly sweeter and milder in flavor than standard green cabbage. You can substitute Napa in almost any recipe calling for cabbage.

get creative

Ginger Lime BBQ Sauce

1 TB Canola or Vegetable Oil
½ Cup chopped Red Onion
2 TB minced Fresh Ginger
2 Garlic Cloves, minced
½ Cup (Your Choice) Mustard Based BBQ Sauce
1 TB Lime Juice and 1 TB Honey

In a large skillet, sauté the red onion in the vegetable oil for 3 minutes. Add the ginger and garlic - sauté for a minute longer. Remove from the heat. Add the BBQ sauce to a bowl and mix in the sautéed vegetables, vinegar and honey.

Tasty Wine Tip

E. Guigal Cotes du Rhone Rose 🍇 *Rhone, France*
Total Wine about $12.00

This lovely pink wine from one of France's wine giants is a delicious cool match for the Asian grill. Made from a blend of Grenache, Cinsault, Mourvedre and Syrah, it's crisp strawberry and cherry flavors combine with a smooth texture and a dry finish to make this a refreshing summertime quaff.

North African Chicken
and Chickpeas

I loved cooking, teaching, learning and eating in Africa. My meals were loaded with incredibly beautiful fruits, veggies, beans and grains. And the influence of diverse cultures is expressed through the use of spices. This is a recipe guaranteed to make even the most skeptical curry eater a believer. Even if you don't think you like curry – try making the Ras el Hanout. It's a little sweeter than other curry powders, and creates an authentic and aromatic dinner.

 *Flexitarian*

2 TB Olive Oil
2 Cups chopped Yellow Onion
1 TB Curry Powder
2 grated Garlic Cloves
4 Boneless, Skinless Chicken Breasts,
   cut in half horizontally
Sea Salt and Pepper
1 Lemon, Juiced (2 -3 TB)
1 Cup Low Salt/Fat Chicken Stock
1 Can Chickpeas (15 oz), drained and well rinsed
½ Cup Plain Fat Free Greek Yogurt
½ Cup chopped Cilantro
Lemon Slices for garnish

Taste and Savor TV: Chopping Onions, Grating Garlic and Ginger, Chopping Herbs, Cutting Chicken

Kitchen Smidgen

Chickpeas are just another name for Garbanzo Beans. They are enjoyed in many cuisines, and are called by different names depending on where they are used - including ceci, channa and Bengal gram, Around since prehistoric times, chickpeas are "nutty" tasting and packed with fiber, folate, zinc and protein.

get creative

Curry powder is not just one spice, but a mixture of many different spices. For an African twist on Curry Powder, try making Ras el Hanout: Stir together 1 Tsp each: Nutmeg, Salt, Pepper, Ginger and Cumin, then add ½ Tsp each Mace, Allspice and Cinnamon. Ras el Hanout means in Arabic "top of the shop" and refers to a mixture of the best spices a seller has to offer.

Step One
In a medium skillet, heat the olive oil. Add the onions and the curry powder, cook and stir for 5 minutes until softened. Add the garlic and cook for 1 minute.

Step Two
Season the chicken with salt and pepper. Add to the onion mixture and sauté until browned. Add the lemon juice, chicken stock, and chickpeas to the pan. Cook and stir for 20 minutes over medium heat, or until chicken is cooked through and the sauce is reduced.

Step Three
Remove from the heat, stir in the yogurt and cilantro, and add the lemon slices as garnish. Serve over brown rice or couscous that has been prepared with golden raisins and toasted almonds.

Tasty Wine Tip

ONO - Viognier, Riesling, Chardonnay  *Rapel Valley, Chile*
Total Wine about $15.00

From the foothills of the Andes Mountains, here's the perfect pairing for curry chicken. It's a delicate blend of 35% Viognier, 35% Riesling and 30% Chardonnay that smells of tropical fruit and apricots and tastes of crisp citrus, peaches and cream. ONO is an ancient name in Chile and speaks to Anakena vineyards commitment to high quality and conservation of the environment.

Grilled Mustard Maple Chicken with Tarragon

I love the flavor of Maple syrup, don't you? I'm always looking for a new way to incorporate it into cooking – savory dishes as well as sweet. This recipe makes the sweetness of maple, the tanginess of Dijon mustard and the fresh licorice taste of tarragon dance in your mouth! The first time I enjoyed this unusual combo of flavors was in an appetizer at a business reception. It intrigued me, and I came home, experimented until I hit on just the right marriage of maple and mustard. I hope you enjoy it as much as we do.

 *Flexitarian*

Marinade

¼ Cup Spicy Whole Grain Mustard
2 TB Lemon Juice
2 Tsp Worcestershire Sauce
1 Tsp minced Tarragon
¼ Tsp Black Pepper

4 Boneless Skinless Chicken Breasts
 – halved horizontally

Sauce

½ Cup Spicy Whole Grain Mustard
¼ Cup Lemon Juice
2 – 4 TB Maple Syrup
1 TB Worcestershire Sauce
1 TB minced Tarragon
Dash of Cayenne Pepper
¼ Tsp Black Pepper
½ Tsp Sea Salt
Chopped Fresh Tarragon for garnish

 Taste and Savor TV: Cutting Chicken

Kitchen Smidgen

When buying tarragon, make sure you buy French tarragon instead of Russian. French tarragon is extremely fragrant with a pronounced anise flavor. Yet another tarragon variety – often called Mexican tarragon - can stand in for the French in a pinch, but is a little "spicier". Tarragon's species name , dracunculus, comes from the Latin for dragon, and reflects the shape of its leaves as well as its Middle Ages reputation for curing snake bites.

get creative

You probably know that maple syrup is a delicious sweetener made from the sap of maple trees. But did you know that it's available in different grades from AA though D? Grade A is sold widely and typically served with pancakes or breakfast. Grade B is my favorite, darker with a little more intense flavor; it's worth the work to seek it out! Try your own taste test to discover which one you like.

Step One
Whisk together the marinade ingredients in a large bowl. Add the chicken and mix well. Cover and Marinate for up to 1 hour.

Step Two
Mix the sauce ingredients together and place in a small saucepan over medium heat and warm for about 10 minutes.

Step Three
Remove the chicken from the marinade and pat dry. Grill over medium heat for 5 - 7 minutes. Turn it only once during cooking. Remove, dunk in the warm sauce and garnish with tarragon.

Tasty Wine Tip
George Duboeuf Fleurie, Flower Label, Beaujolais  *Fleurie, France*
Total Wine about $15.00

This flavorful wine is from maker Georges Duboeuf, who has been called the "king" of Gamay. Gamay is the primary grape grown in Beaujolais. Fleurie is one of the top ten wine areas or "Crus" in Beaujolais. It has potent aroma of ripe strawberries and cherries and a juicy taste to match.

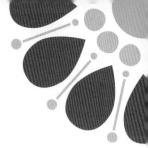

Chicken Braised with White Wine and Creamy Manchego Polenta

*I developed this recipe for the annual luncheon of the "Angels on Earth",
a wonderful organization of dynamic women who provide funds and
gifts for cancer patients. Jillian Pritchard Cooke, the founder and
inspiration for the organization loves all things French. This dish is a
riff on a Provencal Gardiane, or a stew made with chicken or beef and
vegetables. It's a super make-ahead meal. It's even better when you cook
the stew the day before, pop in the fridge and reheat it.*

1 Cup Whole Wheat Flour
1 TB each Salt and Pepper, plus
   more to taste
8 Boneless Skinless Chicken Thighs
3 TB Olive Oil
1 Large Yellow Onion, diced
1 Large Red Pepper, diced
16 Oz. Crimini Mushrooms, sliced
4 Cloves Garlic, grated or minced
2 TB Herbes de Provence
3/4 Cup Dry White Wine
1 (28 Oz.) Can chopped Tomatoes
3 TB chopped Fresh Oregano

Flexitarian

Chicken Braised with White Wine and Creamy Manchego Polenta

Step One
Preheat the oven to 350°F. Place the flour, salt and pepper in a plastic zippy bag, add the chicken and shake to coat the pieces. Heat the oil over medium high in a large ovenproof dutch oven. Add the chicken and brown the pieces, removing them when golden.

Step Two
Add the onion and red pepper to the pot, and cook and stir until the onions are soft. Add the mushrooms and cook until the juices have evaporated. Add the garlic, herbes de provence, the white wine and tomatoes. Return the chicken to the pot, burying the pieces in the vegetable mixture.

Step Three
Bring the dish to a full simmer, cover and place in the oven. Cook for 30 minutes or until the chicken is tender. Sprinkle with oregano and serve on top of:

Creamy Manchego Polenta
4 Cups each, Water and Nonfat Milk
2 Cups Quick Cooking Polenta
6 Oz Manchego, shredded
Sea Salt and Pepper to taste

Bring the water and milk to a boil on top of the stove and sprinkle the polenta into the liquid, whisking constantly. When the polenta begins to thicken, stir in the cheese. Remove from the heat and taste for salt and pepper.

Kitchen Smidgen

Crimini mushrooms, originally from Italy, are closely related to the common white mushroom. Large Criminis are called Portabellas. Seen "Baby Bellas" in the grocery store? They are Crimini mushrooms that have been "rebranded" for marketing to the American public.

get creative

Invented in the 1970s, Herbes de Provence is a combination of savory, basil, fennel, thyme and lavender along with other herbs. Great for grilling, it also adds a Mediterranean flair to stews and braises.

 Taste and Savor TV: Chopping Onions

Tasty Wine Tip

Borsao **Northeast Spain,**
Cost Plus World Market about $8.00

This delicious wine, a blend of mostly garnacha, (grenache) shows just how delicious a light and fruity red can be. You'll enjoy the taste of bright red berries, with vanilla and a little touch of spice. At only $8 a bottle, it is the perfect with a weeknight burger or a roasted chicken.

California Chicken Saltimbocca

When you serve your entree rolled and sliced, the dish inspires oohs and ahhs. Try pounding a chicken breast or a boneless pork chop and stuff it with you favorite veggies and a little cheese – instant professional presentation! This chicken and veggie dish was the entrée for one of my Taste Club classes about California Central Coast wines. My friend, photographer Lynn Stowe, graciously took glamour shots of the dinner, and joined in the fun.

 *Flexitarian*

2 TBs Each, minced Fresh Rosemary, and minced Fresh Sage
1 Tsp Fresh Thyme
4 Boneless Skinless Chicken Breasts, cut in half horizontally
8 Slices Prosciutto
2 TB Olive Oil
Sea Salt and Pepper to taste
1 Cup Dry White Wine
2 TB Lemon Juice

Step One

Lay the chicken breasts out on a cutting board. Cover each breast with a slice of Prosciutto and a sprinkle of herbs. Roll up each breast and tie with kitchen twine. Season with salt and pepper.

Step Two

Heat the oil in a large sauté pan over medium high. Place the chicken in the pan and sauté until golden brown. Add the wine and lemon juice, cover and simmer on low for 20 minutes or until cooked through. Serve with the herb roasted veggies.

Taste and Savor TV: Cutting Chicken, Grating Garlic and Ginger, Chopping Herbs

Kitchen Smidgen

Layers of flavor are created by using dried herbs when you roast the vegetables, and then sprinkle your dish with the fresh herbs when it comes out of the oven.

get creative

Make sure to use Kitchen Twine to tie up the chicken rolls. You can buy it in a home goods store - or at the hardware store! Just make sure it is 100% Cotton Twine.

Herb Rubbed Veggies

3 Cups sliced Zucchini
2 Cut Red Peppers
2 Cups sliced Yellow Squash
2 Red Onions, quartered
1 Large Head Fennel, sliced
3 TB Balsamic Vinegar
2 TB Olive Oil
½ Tsp EACH, Dried: Basil, Oregano, Tarragon, Thyme, Parsley, Rosemary,
Salt and Pepper
4 Garlic Cloves, grated
Chopped Fresh Herbs for garnish

Preheat the oven to 425°F. Toss the veggies, vinegar, oil, dried herbs, salt and pepper together in a baking dish. Cover and roast for 45 minutes or until tender and beginning to brown. Toss them with the fresh herbs and serve.

Tasty Wine Tip

Hahn Meritage   *California Central Coast*
Publix about $15.00

Red Wine with Chicken? Yes! Meritage is the name used in California for a classic Bordeaux blend of Merlot, Cabernet Sauvignon, Petit Verdot, Malbec, and Cabernet Franc. Deep dark red color with toasty oak, blackberry and spicy vanilla flavors make it a great pair for the herb roasted chicken and vegetables.

Chicken Masala with
Lemon Raita

*My family loves Indian food. My sister and brother-in-law spent 3
years living in India, and I was the lucky recipient of many cooking
lessons from this incredibly flavorful cuisine. I often tell people who
claim not to like it – they haven't eaten good Indian food yet. My
friend Kristen, owns a wonderful spice company called "Modern
Day Masala". Her spices are often the inspiration for my frequent
forays into Indian food. Try this easy take on an Indian chicken
favorite and I guarantee you'll be serving it again and again.*

 *Flexitarian*

2 Cucumbers, peeled and seeded
2 TB Coriander Seeds
2 TB Cumin Seeds
2 TB Fennel Seeds
2 TB Olive Oil, divided
6 Boneless Skinless Chicken Breasts, cut in half horizontally
2 TB olive oil
1 Tsp Each Sea Salt and Pepper
2 Cups Nonfat Greek Yogurt
1 TB Lemon Zest + 1 TB Lemon Juice
1 Clove Garlic, minced
1/8 Tsp Cayenne Pepper
1 Head Napa Cabbage, shredded
Freshly chopped Cilantro to garnish

Kitchen Smidgen

Masala is a word that indicates a combination of spices ground into a powder or
paste that is used in Indian cooking or it can also mean "dish flavored with a
spice mixture".

get creative

If you haven't tried Greek yogurt, you are missing a real treat. Thicker and creamier than other yogurt, it is made by removing the whey, (liquid) from the solids. You can make Greek-style yogurt by placing regular yogurt in a coffee filter and letting it drain for an hour or so to remove the liquid.

 *Taste and Savor TV:* Cutting Chicken

Step One
Preheat the oven to 350°F. Shred the cucumber and lightly salt. Place in a strainer to drain for at least 15 minutes.

Step Two
To make the masala, toast the coriander, cumin and fennel seeds in a dry skillet over medium heat until fragrant - 3 to 4 minutes. Remove from the heat, let cool and grind in a coffee or spice grinder.

Step Three
Brush the chicken with 1 TB olive oil - season lightly with salt and pepper. Sprinkle all but 2 Tsp of the masala over the chicken breasts.

Step Four
Heat the remaining TB of oil in a large skillet. Add the chicken to the skillet and sauté for about 3 minutes on each side. Transfer to the oven to complete cooking for 6 to 8 minutes or until done.

Step Five
While the chicken is cooking, transfer the cucumber to a bowl and stir in the yogurt, zest and juice, garlic, cayenne and the 2 Tsp of the spice mixture. Serve the cabbage topped with the chicken and lemon raita, garnished with cilantro.

Tasty Wine Tip
Sula Chenin Blanc 🍇 *Nashik, India,*
Whole Foods about $13.00

Wine from India? Yes! This Chenin Blanc is a perfect compliment for the masala and tangy lemon raita.It has an appealing nose of green apples and lychees and a light taste with a good citrus balance and a touch of minerality. Check it out and see if you agree!

Sherry Vinegar Chicken and Warm Spanish Potato Salad

Tangy chicken, warm potatoes and veggies – it doesn't get better much than this. The new and interesting wines of Spain have motivated me to investigate the lively and appealing foods of this diverse country - and the smoked paprika. If you haven't tried this spice, now is the time. One of my favorite descriptions of this spice is one given to me while teaching a veggie class. A student, when smelling it said, "Nancy, it smells like bacon without bacon." And, it does. Next time you are looking to ramp up the savory, smoky element in a dish, break out the smoked paprika!

 *Flexitarian*

Sherry Vinegar Chicken

2 Large Chicken Breasts
  Cut in half horizontally
½ Cup Sherry Vinegar
Sea Salt and Black Pepper
2 TB Olive Oil

Place the chicken in a zippy bag with the vinegar and oil for at least 30 minutes - but not more than 2 hours. Remove, pat dry and sprinkle with salt and pepper. Grill for about 5 minutes on each side, or until chicken juices run clear when pierced.

Spanish Potato Salad

1.5 LBs Assorted Fingerling
  Potatoes, cut in 2 inch pieces
1 TB Sea Salt
½ TB Ground Cumin
1 TB Smoked Sweet Paprika
½ TB Chili Powder
½ TB each Sea Salt and Pepper
1 TB Dijon Mustard
2 TB Sherry Vinegar
¼ Cup Extra Virgin Olive Oil
½ Small Red Onion, thinly sliced
1 Cup thinly sliced Celery
¼ Cup chopped Cilantro
½ Cup chopped Green Olives

Kitchen Smidgen

Most Fingerling Potatoes are a "heritage variety" of potatoes. "Heritage potatoes" are those grown from seeds 50 to 100 years old. Fun to use because of their unusual shapes and colors, they are best boiled, steamed or baked.

get creative

Use different types of vinegars as a marinade for chicken or pork.
Raspberry vinegar makes a wonderful chicken marinade.
Turn it into dinner: make a salad with baby lettuces, fresh or
dried berries, goat cheese and toasted slivered almonds.
Toss with raspberry vinaigrette and top with raspberry
vinegar marinated chicken.

Step One

Place the potatoes in a saucepan, cover with water and bring to a boil. Add the salt and cook 12 minutes or until just tender.

Step Two

While the potatoes are cooking, combine the cumin, paprika, chili powder, salt and pepper. Whisk in the mustard, vinegar and olive oil. Add the onion, celery, cilantro and olives. Drain the potatoes and add to the salad. Serve warm.

 *Taste and Savor TV:* Cutting Chicken

Tasty Wine Tip

Castle Rock Pinot Noir 2006  *Mendocino, California*
Total Wine about $10

A big bright aroma with berries, spice and a velvety plush taste of red fruit make this Spanish wine a real charmer. Tempranillo is an indigenous grape to Spain, and shares many qualities with Pinot Noir - soft berry and cherry fruit flavors, medium acidity and tannins. You'll enjoy it with Sherry Vinegar Chicken as it stands up well to the strong tastes of grilled meats and smoked paprika.

Southern Pepper Jelly Chicken with Warm Black -Eyed Pea Salsa

I am lucky to have wonderful assistants and friends at Cooks Warehouse who I call "jammers". These artistic folks are always putting up new, delicious and different jams, jellies, butters and chutneys. The jammers inspire lots of creativity in me; I am always looking for a way to use their savory and sweet products in new recipes. Here's a Southern-style combination I think you will like no matter where in the world you are making dinner tonight. Sautéed chicken accompanied by black-eyed pea salsa made with tangy pepper jelly. And, if you love the salsa like I do, use it as a delicious chip dip, too!

Southern Pepper Jelly Chicken

1 TB Olive Oil, divided
4 Boneless Skinless Chicken Breasts
Salt and Black Pepper to taste
2 Cloves Garlic, grated
½ Tsp Red Pepper Flakes
¼ Cup White Wine (or Apple Cider)
½ Cup Pepper Jelly
¼ Cup Stone Ground Dijon Mustard

Step One

Heat half the olive oil over medium heat in a sauté pan with lid. Season the chicken with salt and pepper, then sauté until just golden. Remove from the pan and set aside.

Step Two

Heat the remaining oil, add the garlic and red pepper flakes. Cook and stir for one minute. Add the wine, jelly and mustard. Stir and cook until melted.

Step Three

Return the chicken to the pan, cover with the lid and finish cooking in the sauce. Remove and set aside while you make:

Kitchen Smidgen

Make sure to buy cookware that is heavy for it's size, and well constructed. Good pots and pans should last a lifetime!

get creative

If you are watching fats and calories in the new year, try using smoked turkey when recipes call for ham or bacon. It will give you a similar smoky, meaty taste.

📺 *Taste and Savor TV:*
Cutting Chicken, Grating Garlic and Ginger,
Chopping Onions, Chopping Herbs

Warm Black-eyed Pea Salsa

1 Tsp Olive Oil
½ Cup chopped County Ham or Smoked Turkey
1 Cup minced Red Onion
2 Cloves Garlic, grated
1 Tsp Ground Cumin
¼ Tsp Freshly Cracked Black Pepper
1 (16 oz) Bag Frozen Black Eyed Peas, prepared as package directs
1 (14 ½ oz) Can chopped Tomatoes
½ Cup minced Fresh Cilantro
¾ Cup chopped Sweet Cherry Peppers

Salt and Black Pepper to taste. Heat the olive oil over medium heat and sauté the ham until just brown, add the onion, cook and stir for 3 – 5 minutes. Add the garlic. Stir in the cumin, pepper, peas and tomatoes and bring to a boil. Remove from the heat and stir in cilantro and peppers. Season to taste with salt and pepper.

Flexitarian

Tasty Wine Tip

Torres 2006 Celeste Red 7:00 PM   *Ribera del Duero, Spain*
Cost Plus World Market about $12.00

Ribera del Duero is known for its amazing Tempranillo and this one is no exception – it's full of the delicious aroma and taste of cherries and herbs. On the label, Celeste is from celestial skies, and 7:00 PM reflects the red color of the Ribera Del Duero sky at 7.

Enchiladas with
Peanut Almond Sauce

*Who says you can't make healthy Mexican Food? This delectable
dish is a perfect example of the rich spicy cuisine from South
of the Border – without a lot of fat and calories. And you can
change this recipe from Flexitarian to Vegetarian without a
lot of fuss. Just substitute veg broth for the chicken broth and
frozen spinach for the chicken breasts. Now you have a dish that
pleases everyone loaded with veggies, spice and crunch.*

 *Flexitarian*

1 Cup Raw Whole Almonds

6 Dried Ancho Chili Peppers, seeded, cut into pieces

3 TB White Sesame Seeds

1 Cup Roasted, Salted Peanuts

½ Red Onion, coarsely chopped

2 Cloves Garlic

1 Slice Whole Wheat Bread, dipped in Apple Cider Vinegar, drained

2-3 Cups Chicken (or Veg) Broth

18 Corn Tortillas

2 Large Cooked Chicken Breasts, shredded - or 3 Boxes Frozen Spinach,
defrosted, drained well

½ Cup chopped Roasted Peanuts

Chopped Cilantro

 Taste and Savor TV: Chopping Onions

Kitchen Smidgen

Ancho Chili Peppers are Dried Poblanos. Look for ones that are still supple and pliable
- they should smell like spicy raisins. Remove the seeds and stems, and cut
them into pieces with kitchen shears.

get creative

The whole wheat bread dipped in vinegar is a way to add texture and flavor to the sauce. This technique is also used in delicious red-pepper-filled Spanish Romesco Sauce!

Step One
Preheat the oven to 350°F. Toast the almonds on a sheet pan for 8 minutes. While the almonds are toasting, in a skillet over medium high heat toast the chilies and sesame seeds until the seeds are golden, about 3 minutes.

Step Two
In a food processor, grind the peanuts and almonds, sesame seeds and chilies. Add the onion, garlic and bread and 2 cups of the broth. Puree.

Step Three
Add the puree to the skillet. Bring to a simmer over medium heat to blend the flavors. Cook and stir for 5 minutes. (If mixture is too thick to dip the tortillas, add more broth.)

Step Four
Warm the tortillas briefly in the microwave and dip them, one at a time into the nut puree - fill with 2 TB of the chicken (or spinach). Fold in half and place in a 9" X 12" baking pan. Spread the remaining sauce over the top, and bake for 20 minutes. Garnish with chopped peanuts and cilantro to serve.

Tasty Wine Tip
Annie's Lane Chardonnay   *Clare Valley, Australia*
Cost Plus World Market about $10.00

This lively, clean, green Chardonnay, with flavors of peaches and melons, is a palatable pairing for lightly spicy Mexican dishes. It's rich mouth-filling feel is due to a method of vinification called malolactic fermentation that creates a buttery body and more taste complexity in the wine.

Churrasco Style Steak with Chimichurri

If I am going to eat steak – it has to be really good. This recipe qualifies! Even if you are not a meat eater, you'll love the Churrasco rub on cod, halibut or any firm textured fish or tofu. Add the Chimichurri sauce and lots of lemon, a crisp green salad with simple vinaigrette and dinner is done.

 *Flexitarian*

2 LBs Sirloin cut into 2" chunks
1 Recipe Churrasco-style Dry Rub
1 Recipe Chimichurri
Grilled Bread for serving if desired

Step One
Place the steak in a plastic zip bag and add ¼ - ½ cup of the dry rub. Close the bag and massage to coat the meat. Leave in the fridge 1 hour or up to overnight.

Step Two
Remove the steak from the fridge for ½ hour before grilling and load onto bamboo skewers. Preheat your grill, (or grill pan), on high, and cook over medium high heat until desired doneness. (For medium rare, cook for about 4 minutes per side). Garnish with a drizzle of Chimichurri.

Kitchen Smidgen

Chimichurri is a green sauce which is also used as a marinade for grilled meat. It is originally from Argentina and Uruguay. Just like curry in India, each family has its own unique blend of ingredients. Chimichurri reflects influences from Argentina's and Uruguay's many cultures including Spanish and Italian.

get creative

Churrasco is a Portuguese and Spanish word for beef or grilled meat. A different cut of meat is the distinction for countries from Europe to Latin American to Africa that serve Churrasco. In Argentina and Brazil, this BBQ was traditionally served on the ranch each night for dinner, with a twice a year special event that invited the local community. Try hosting your own Churrasco inspired BBQ!

Churrasco-style Dry Rub

2 Tsp Each Salt and Pepper
2 TB Garlic Powder
2 TB Smoked Paprika
2 Tsp Ground Cumin
4 TB Dark Brown Sugar

Mix all the spices together in a bowl. Add the brown sugar and mix thoroughly.

Chimichurri

1 Cup Parsley, (packed)
½ Cup Extra Virgin Olive Oil
½ Cup Cilantro, (packed)
⅓ Cup Red Wine Vinegar
2 Cloves Garlic, peeled
¾ Tsp Red Pepper Flakes
½ Tsp Cumin
½ Tsp Salt

Combine all the ingredients in a food processor or blender and blend well. Set aside for at least 2 hours before serving.

Tasty Wine Tip

Tilia Malbac   *Eastern Mendoza, Argentina*
Costco about $11.00

Malbac, historically from France, has made a delicious home in Argentina. Deep purple Tilia offers not only a rich black cherry aroma and taste, but it is a fantastic value for such a flavorful BBQ partner.

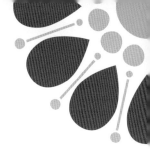

Ginger Sesame Fish

Here's one of those recipes that are too easy to be true – one package for each diner – and no pans to wash. This recipe was inspired by my "oldest" friend, Donna. We lived together as flight attendants, and just like today – she loves to eat, avoids cooking with more than 5 ingredients and hates recipes with lots of cleanup. I hope you like this dish as much as she Donna does!

4 Fish Filets (8-10 oz each)
4 Cups Cooked Brown Rice
2 Cups shredded Napa Cabbage
2 Cups shredded Carrots
6 Green Onions, White and Green thinly sliced
3 TB Canola or Grape Seed Oil
2 TB grated Fresh Ginger
3 Cloves Garlic, grated
4 TB Light Soy Sauce
5 Tsp Dark Sesame Oil
¼ Cup chopped Cilantro
Aluminum Foil

Pescetarian

Ginger Sesame Fish

Step One

Preheat the oven to 425°F Make 8 foil squares about 16" x 16". On each foil square, spread ⅛ of the rice. Cut each fish filet in half. Layer the fish, cabbage, carrots, and scallions on the rice.

Step Two

In a small bowl, whisk the oil, ginger, garlic, soy sauce, sesame oil and cilantro together. Pour over the fish. Close up the packets by crimping the edges together. Bake 20-25 minutes. The easiest way to grate the ginger and garlic is with a Microplane.

 Taste and Savor TV: Grating Garlic and Ginger, Chopping Herbs

Kitchen Smidgen

This recipe uses aluminum foil to create an oven package for the rice, fish and veggies. When you see the words "en papillote" it is the same cooking method as we are using here: placing food in a closed package and cooking in the oven or on a grill. You can use foil or parchment paper to make a package.

get creative

You can enjoy just about any type of fish in this recipe. If your favorite fish is not in season, don't hesitate to use frozen fish. Frozen fish is as good as fresh fish, and indeed sometimes better. Fish and seafood begin to decline in quality immediately after being caught. Freezing fish quickly retains quality and seals in freshness. When fish is frozen at sea it could not be fresher.

Tasty Wine Tip

René Barbier Mediterranean White, Catalunya   Penedes, Spain
Cost Plus about $7.00

Simple, Affordable and Refreshing are the three words that describe this light weekday white. This blend of Xarello, Macabeo and Parellada grapes are surprisingly good for sipping with light fish dishes. Never heard of these grapes? Bet you have enjoyed them before - they are the principal grapes of the Spanish sparkling wine, Cava.

Grilled Fish with
North African Spices

Do you have a friend or family member that is a confirmed carnivore? Try this grilled dish with a fresh tuna steak and watch them smile. This blend of spices is super on any fish - it also makes a perfect marinade for pork or chicken.

 *Pescetarian*

2 TB Olive Oil
½ Tsp Pepper
1 Tsp Cumin
1 Tsp Ground Coriander
1 Tsp Turmeric
1 Tsp Smoked Paprika
2 Cloves Garlic
6 Green Onions
½ Cup Cilantro, packed
¼ Cup Parsley, packed
4 Tuna Steaks, or other Fish Steaks or Filets

Kitchen Smidgen

When grilling meat, poultry or fish, it's always a good idea to bring it to room temperature before cooking - it allows the protein to cook evenly, avoiding drying out the exterior before the inside cooks.

get creative

To maximize the flavor of dried spices, toast them in a pan with or without oil. Stir them around until they release their aromas, then remove from the heat so they don't scorch.

Step One

Heat 2 TB Olive Oil in a small sauté pan over medium high heat. Add the pepper, cumin, coriander, turmeric and paprika. Stir for 1 - 2 minutes or until spices are fragrant.

Step Two

Add the garlic to a food processor and pulse until well minced. Add the onions, cilantro and parsley. Add the spiced oil and pulse. Cut the fish lengthwise into ½" slices. Place the fish in a zippy bag, pour the marinade over, and refrigerate for 2 hours.

Step Three

Remove the fish from the fridge 30 minutes before grilling. Using a grill pan, or clean, oiled grill outside, cook the fish until done, (turning once) about 2-3 minutes per side.

Tasty Wine Tip

Domaine/Maison Joseph Drouhin, Beaujolais Villages   *Beaujolais, France*
Total Wine about $13.00

Here's a fun light red to pair with fish like this. Serve this easy drinking, fruit forward red wine a bit chilled to bring out its delicious raspberry-strawberry flavors. Made with the Gamay grape, it hails from the greater Burgundy area of France, in Beaujolais. Carbonic maceration is the traditional method used to create this wine. Grapes are placed in a large vessel to ferment, so most of the juice ferments inside the grapes, resulting in low tannins and fruity bright tastes.

Grilled Salmon with Fresh Pineapple Tomato Salsa

Juicy pineapple and beautiful ripe tomatoes pair to make a yummy salsa to top salmon in this recipe. In the summer, I find myself firing up the grill at least 2 or 3 times a week, most often for fish or fresh-from the-market vegetables. If you're not grilling outside, it makes a perfect grill pan dinner, too! Don't limit this salsa just to salmon. It's super with chicken, pork, or crisp and crunchy chips.

 *Pescetarian*

The Salmon:
4 Salmon Filets
2 TB Low Sodium Soy Sauce

The Salsa:
1½ Cup chopped Fresh Pineapple
1 Cup chopped Ripe Tomato
½ Cup chopped Red Onion
¼ Cup chopped Red Bell Pepper
Juice and Zest of 1 Lime
1 Jalapeno, chopped with Seeds and Ribs removed
½ Tsp Sea Salt
1 TB Extra Virgin Olive Oil
¼ Cup chopped Cilantro

Make the Salsa by mixing all the ingredients together. Set aside to allow the flavors to blend. Prepare the salmon by placing it in a zippy bag with the soy sauce while the grill heats. (Don't leave it too long - after about 30 minutes the soy sauce will "cook" your salmon!) With a set of tongs, prepare your grill grates with a paper towel dipped in oil. Preheat your grill for 10 minutes on high, (or get your grill pan hot). Turn the grill to medium and cook the salmon for about 3 minutes per side. Remove and serve topped with the salsa.

Kitchen Smidgen

To cut a fresh pineapple in chunks - first take off the top and bottom, so it stands upright on the counter. Then working from top to bottom, slice down on the outside - following the curve of the fruit. Now, cut it in quarters and remove and discard the tough core, and chop the sweet flesh.

get creative

And use the grill for dessert, too. Peel and pit 4 peaches.
Cook them on the grill until nicely brown on the edges.
Remove, slice and serve over frozen vanilla yogurt
topped with crushed gingersnaps.

Taste and Savor TV:
Chopping Onions

Tasty Wine Tip

Castle Rock Pinot Noir 2006   *Mendocino, California*
Total Wine about $10

The rich earthy taste of soy sauce paired with the bright flavors of pineapple salsa make Pinot Noir a good choice for this dinner. Red wine from France named "Burgundy" is made from the Pinot Noir grape. You'll find aromas of red cherries, tea and spices on the nose, and it tastes like plums and strawberries with just a hint of vanilla. Pinot Noir is typically more expensive - this one is a good value for the money.

Grilled Salmon
Sesame Sliders

These salmon sliders are not only delicious – they are gorgeous, too! Super easy to prepare, you can make them the day before, pop them in the fridge and they will be ready for the party tomorrow.

 *Pescetarian*

1 Large Egg
1 TB Soy Sauce
2 Tsp toasted Sesame Oil
1 LB Skinless Salmon Fillet, cut into ⅛ dice
¾ Cup Whole Wheat Panko Crumbs
¼ Cup thinly sliced Green Onions
2 TBs Sesame Seeds
Oil for Brushing the Grill
Wasabi Mayonnaise
Lettuce Cups or Whole Wheat Slider Buns
Chopped Cilantro

Step One
In a medium bowl, whisk together the egg, soy sauce and sesame oil. Add the salmon, the panko, green onions, sesame seeds and mix. Form into 2" wide and ½" tall patties. Cover and chill for at least 1 hour.

Step Two
Preheat your oiled grill pan, (or a clean oiled grill outside), and over medium heat, cook the salmon sliders on one side for about 2-3 minutes. Turn, and cook for an additional 2 minutes (or until they are cooked as much as you like).

Step Three
Place each slider in a lettuce cup and top with Wasabi Mayo, or place in a grilled whole wheat bun along with shredded napa cabbage. Garnish with chopped cilantro.

Kitchen Smidgen

Wasabi Mayo is super easy to make. Just buy a tube of wasabi horseradish from the sushi bar at your local grocery store. Start with about a tsp and mix it into ½ cup of low fat mayo. Taste and add more wasabi as desired.

get creative

Sesame is an annual plant that grows about 3 ½ feet tall. Whether its seeds are black, tan or white, whole, ground into a paste or pressed for oil, sesame probably originated in Africa and is now grown mostly in India, China, Mexico, and the Sudan. Did you know that you should store sesame seeds and opened sesame products in the fridge? With their high oil content, they can spoil quickly. Try topping your salads and stir fries with a combination of white and black seeds for variety, color and flavor.

Tasty Wine Tip

Cape Indaba Chardonnay — *Western Cape, South Africa,*
Cost Plus World Market about $9.00

Here's an easy drinking white wine that you can buy for the whole party. Great chilled in an ice bucket on the patio – or straight from the fridge, this South African crisp quaffer is super with grilled seafood. Offering aromas of tropical fruit and peaches, Indaba has a nice balance of tastes including green apples and lemon and has a finish with good acidity.

Seared Serrano Wrapped Halibut with Romesco Sauce

Serrano is one of my most requested sauces. I have been heard to say that "it would make packing peanuts taste good"! An old world style sauce, it is thickened with bread instead of flour or cornstarch, which gives it a delicious hearty texture. Just like Balsamic vinegar is a well-known condiment from Italy, Sherry vinegar is Spain's delicious export that gives this sauce a delightful zing!

Flexitarian

Romesco Sauce

1 Cup Slivered Almonds

2 1" Slices Rustic Country Bread

½ Cup Sherry Vinegar

2 Roasted Red Peppers

2 TB Tomato Paste

1 TB Fresh Lemon Juice

1 TB Sweet Smoked Paprika

½ Tsp each Salt and Black Pepper

¾ Cup Extra Virgin Olive Oil

Step One
On a baking sheet, toast the almonds in a 350°F oven for 10 minutes. Set aside to cool.

Step Two
Cube the bread, and place in a bowl with the vinegar for 30 minutes.

Step Three
In a food processor, grind the almonds, add the vinegar and bread, the peppers, tomato paste, lemon juice, paprika, salt and pepper. With the motor running, slowly add the olive oil. Taste for salt and pepper.

Kitchen Smidgen

Serrano (Mountain) Ham is a type of dry cured Spanish ham, which is usually served in thin slices just like Italian prosciutto. Serrano is widely available, but if you can't find it, feel free to use thinly sliced prosciutto.

get creative

Can't find Halibut at the store this week? Discover a Great Sale? Substitute another white fish in this recipe: Cod, Grouper, Monkfish, or close "fishy" relative, Turbot.

 *Taste and Savor TV:*
Roasting Red Peppers

Halibut

4 Halibut Filets

4 Slices Serrano Ham, thinly sliced

1 Tsp Each Sea Salt and Pepper

1 Tsp Sweet Smoked Paprika

1 Tsp Olive Oil

Step One
Prepare the halibut by wrapping each filet with a slice of serrano ham around the middle. Sprinkle each filet with salt, pepper and paprika.

Step Two
Heat the olive oil in a heavy skillet over medium high heat.

Step Three
Sear the filets on one side, then the other in the skillet - about 3 minutes per side. Slide into a 350°F oven to finish cooking.

Tasty Wine Tip
Rene Barbier Mediterranean Red  *Catalonia, Spain*
Trader Joes about $6.00

Red Wine with Fish? Yes! The strong flavors in the Romesco and the Serrano call for a red wine. Don't judge this wine by the price, it's similar to wines served everyday in Spain. Mediterranean Red hails from the northeast Catalonia region and is made with Tempranillo, Garnacha and Monastrell grapes. Enjoy a big whiff, and you'll find dark fruit and green herbs, and take a big taste of strawberries, clove and just a little smoke.

Mediterranean Shrimp
with Orzo and Dill

Warm or cold, this dish is a hit. Dill provides a punch of crispness, and the fresh fennel and tomatoes bring lots of color and antioxidants to this party of flavors for your mouth. Creamy, tangy feta and crunchy green onions round out the dish. If you can find whole wheat orzo – it's a great addition.

 *Pescetarian*

The Vinaigrette
¼ Cup chopped Fresh Dill, plus
    extra for garnish
¼ Cup White Wine Vinegar
3 TB Dijon Mustard
½ Cup Olive Oil, plus additional
    for brushing shrimp
Salt and Freshly Ground Pepper

The Orzo
1 LB Orzo, Cooked according to
    package directions
½ Head Fennel, finely chopped
3 Green Onions, thinly sliced
1 Pint Grape Tomatoes, halved
1 Cup Crumbled Feta Cheese
16 Large Shrimp, peeled

Step One
Make the vinaigrette by placing the dill, vinegar, and mustard in a food processor or blender and blending until smooth. With the motor running, slowly add the olive oil and blend until emulsified. Season with salt and pepper to taste.

Step Two
Add the first 4 orzo ingredients to a large bowl. Pour the vinaigrette over the orzo mixture and stir well to combine. Gently fold in the feta cheese.

Step Three
Preheat the grill or a grillpan on high. Brush shrimp with oil and season with salt and pepper. Grill for 1-2 minutes per side or until just cooked through. Place the orzo on plates and top with the shrimp. Garnish with additional dill.

Kitchen Smidgen

Dill is a versatile soft leaved perennial herb that can be used fresh, as a seed or as dried leaves, called dill weed. It has a unique tangy taste that is especially good with seafood, salads and vegetables.

get creative

Feta is one of the most famous exports of Greece. This semi soft white cheese is made of goat's milk just like Chevre from France. Use it anytime you want strong cheese flavor and a soft texture in your dish. Believe it or not, its salty briny taste is a great partner for sweet watermelon!

Taste and Savor TV:
Chopping Herbs

Tasty Wine Tip

Don David Torrontes 🍇 *Cafayate Valley, Chile*
Cost Plus World Market about $15.00

If you are looking for the perfect grilled seafood partner for the weekend – look no further! This is Argentina's characteristic white grape, and nicely, Torrontes is the name of the wine AND the grape. It's tropical and honey aromas and fresh citrus, lime and peach flavors are balanced with a zingy acidity – making it a refreshing aromatic white for hot summer weather.

Grilled Scallops with Bacon and Baby Lettuce

Baby Lettuce, green peas and shredded carrots are the bed for these delicious scallops. Fast and easy – one dish dinner in about 20 minutes!

Flexitarian

The Dressing
¼ Cup Extra Virgin Olive Oil
2 TB Unseasoned Rice Vinegar
1 Tsp Dijon Mustard
1 TB Thyme Leaves
½ Tsp Sugar
½ Tsp Sea Salt
¼ Tsp Pepper

The Bacon and The Scallops
12 Large Dry Pack Scallops
4 Slices Turkey Bacon

The Greens and Vegetables
1 Package Baby Lettuces
8 oz Pkg Frozen Baby Peas, thawed
1 Carrot, Julienned or shredded

Kitchen Smidgen

At the fish counter, ask for Dry Pack Scallops. Those that are Wet Packed may have absorbed up to 30% of their own weight from water and a "special solution". If you can't find Dry Pack, cut your scallops in half horizontally before cooking, they will cook more evenly and quicker.

get creative

Whip up a quick side of toasted croustades with fresh herb butter. Slice a baguette or other crusty loaf into ½" pieces and cut them in half. Toast them in the oven for 5 minutes per side. To 1 stick of room temp unsalted butter, add 1 TB of fresh thyme leaves, ½ Tsp of sea salt and a few grinds of black pepper. Mash well and place in a ramekin. Now you have dinner!

Step One
Prepare the dressing by shaking the ingredients in a jar.

Step Two
Arrange the lettuce on 4 large dinner plates. Sprinkle the peas and carrots on the lettuce.

Step Three
Heat a grill pan, add the bacon and cook until crisp and brown on both sides. Remove the bacon and drain on a rack. When cool, crumble the bacon. Add the scallops to the pan and cook on high heat for about 2 minutes until browned on one side. Turn them over and cook on the other side. The scallops will be opaque when done – don't overcook them or the scallops will be tough and rubbery.

Step Four
Place the bacon and scallops on the lettuces. Shake the dressing mix again and drizzle each salad with the dressing.

Tasty Wine Tip
Chateau de Campuget ROSE   *Costieres de Nimes AOC, France*
Cost Plus World Market about $11.00

Lovely salmon-pink wine makes the scallops in this salad shine. Very aromatic, you taste raspberries and strawberries with a nice crisp finish. Costieres de Nimes is an area, (AOC) in France that is worthy of a good look around - this screwtop rose proves it.

Herbed Grilled Shrimp
and Lemon Pasta

The unique and fresh flavors of parsley, basil and mint arrive
at your table with in this delicious pasta. Loads of flavor
packed in those fresh little herbs, and no fat or calories!
Amazing isn't it? Add a green salad and some fresh fruit –
it's dinner!

 *Pescetarian*

2 TB Olive Oil

2 TB Grated Garlic

½ Tsp Cayenne Pepper

½ Cup Dry White Wine

2 TB finely chopped Parsley

½ Tsp Sea Salt

½ Tsp Cracked Black Pepper

1 LB Large Shrimp, shelled

1 Package Whole Wheat Pasta

1 Lemon in wedges

2 TB Extra Virgin Olive Oil

½ Cup Parmesan, grated

2 TB chopped Fresh Basil

2 TB chopped Fresh Mint

Kitchen Smidgen

Wondering what kind of Whole Wheat Pasta to buy? My favorite is the Barilla brand.
The key to making good whole wheat pasta is to NOT overcook it. Leave it "al
dente" or just a little firmer than white pasta - it will be nutty and delicious.

get creative

And experiment with olive oils. Just like wine, there is a whole culture of olive oil tasting. Discover what you like: grassy or fruity, peppery or bitter. Choose a "house" olive oil just like you choose a house wine! Feel free to use less expensive olive oil for cooking - it has a higher smoke point. But, always use an extra virgin olive oil for finishing. It's from the first pressing of the olives and has a better taste, color and aroma, and its better for you!

Step One

Combine the olive oil, garlic and cayenne in a saucepan over medium heat. Cook and stir for 30 seconds or until the garlic is soft - but not brown. Add the wine, raise the heat to high and cook until reduced by half. Allow to cool and stir in the parsley.

Step Two

Place the shrimp in a bowl and pour the olive oil mixture over it. Add the salt and pepper. Set aside while you preheat the grill or grill pan for 10 minutes on high.

Step Three

Place the shrimp on the grill or a grill pan and cook until just opaque - about 2-3 minutes.

Step Four

Prepare the pasta as directed on the package. When drained, squeeze the lemon over, toss with the olive oil, cheese, basil and mint. Top with shrimp and serve.

Tasty Wine Tip

Sauvion Muscadet Sevre et Maine Sur Lie   *Loire Valley, France*
Total Wine about $10.00

Muscadet (mus-ka-DAY) is the perfect refreshing wine for this spicy, herb-y shrimp pasta. This dry white from the Loire Valley in France is the traditional match for fresh shellfish. You'll find it crisp, citrusy and refreshing. It has been aged "Sur Lie" or on its yeasts, which provides additional flavor and complexity to this just-right summer wine.

Savory Asian Shrimp Wraps

Everyone likes to roll their own food – children especially! This is one of my favorite family dinners, whether I'm serving kindergartners or the senior set. It's so much fun to customize each and every mouthful. If you don't want to roll the flavorful shrimp in lettuce, they are also excellent on rice, or as an appetizer on skewers.

 *Pescetarian*

2 LB Large Shrimp, peeled
2 Jalapenos, Ribs and Seeds removed
½ Cup Fresh Lime Juice
Zest of a Lime
¼ Cup chopped Cilantro
¼ Cup chopped Parsley
2 Garlic Cloves
½ Cup Olive Oil
Sea Salt to taste
½ Cup chopped Peanuts
2 Heads Butter Lettuce

Step One
Remove the Shrimp from your Brine, (if using),and pat dry. Make a marinade for the shrimp by blending in your food processor: the jalepenos, lime juice, zest, cilantro, parsley, and garlic. Slowly drizzle in the olive oil. Spoon it into a zippy bag and add the shrimp. Place in the fridge for a couple of hours.

Step Two
Preheat your gas grill on high. (Or get your grill pan really hot!) Remove the shrimp and discard the marinade. Grill the shrimp for 1- 2 minutes per side, remove, and sprinkle the shrimp with salt. On 4 plates, place the shrimp, some butter lettuce and chopped peanuts.

Kitchen Smidgen
You can improve the flavor and texture of almost any shrimp by brining them! In a large bowl, add 1 Cup Salt and ½ Cup Sugar to 2 Cups Boiling Water. Fill the bowl with ice cubes. Add your shrimp, place in the fridge about 2 hours. Remove, rinse well, and use in any recipe calling for shrimp.

get creative

Serve Fresh Mint Salad with your wraps. In a bowl, place 4 large shredded carrots. Add ½ red onion, cut in very thin slices. In another bowl, combine 2 minced garlic cloves, ¼ cup fish sauce, ½ cup sugar, zest and juice of a lime and ½ of a jalepeno, minced. Toss the first bowl with the second bowl. Set aside for the flavors to blend. Just before serving, toss the salad with 3 TB each chopped fresh mint and basil.

Taste and Savor TV:
Chopping Herbs

Tasty Wine Tip

Martin Codax ALBARINO   *Rias Baixas, Spain 2006*
At Publix about $14.00

If you haven't tried Albarino yet, Savory Asian Shrimp Wraps are the perfect opportunity! Albariño is the name of the wine and the name of the white grape from Rías Baixas in Galicia, in Spain's northwest. You'll smell ripe apricots and taste delicious grapefruit and lemon zest flavors in the glass.

Eastern Shore Crab Cakes

I have so many memories from time spent on the Chesapeake Bay that make me smile or even laugh out loud! This recipe is adapted from my sister's crabcakes recipe, and inspired by Debbie and John's hospitality and joie de vivre. Just thinking about this delicious dish makes me hear the tack against the masts and long for the smell of the fresh clean air. I think you'll think it's heaven on earth when you taste these crabcakes!

 *Pescetarian*

1 LB Back Fin or Lump Crabmeat

2 Tsp EACH Salt and Pepper

¼ Cup Light Mayonnaise

1 Tsp Yellow Mustard

1 Large Egg, Beaten

1 TB Worcestershire Sauce

1 Tsp Old Bay Seasoning

24 Saltine Crackers, Crushed

¼ Cup Dill, minced

2 TB Canola or Vegetable Oil

 Taste and Savor TV: Chopping Herbs

Kitchen Smidgen

Jumbo Lump is the most expensive and largest pieces of crabmeat. Perfect for crab cocktail. Lump – white meat like Jumbo, just a little smaller. Back Fin - Similar to the flavor and texture of Lump, just smaller pieces. Great for crab cakes. Special crabmeat is the smallest pieces of white meat from the crab claw it is the "dark" meat of the crab. Ideal for gratins or seafood stews.

get creative

Old Bay is a traditional Eastern Shore favorite. A spice mix that includes celery salt, paprika, cinnamon, ginger, mustard seed, black and red pepper, it tastes great in crab cakes and as a seasoning for many other savory foods!

Step One
Place the crabmeat in a bowl and add the salt and pepper.

Step Two
In another bowl; mix the mayo, mustard, egg, Worcestershire and Old Bay. Gently fold mixture into crabmeat. Now, toss the dill and ¼ cup Saltines together. Fold into the crabmeat mixture.

Step Three
Place the remainder of the saltines on a plate. Make 4 large crab cakes and lightly coat with the crackers. Place them in the fridge for at least 1 hour.

Step Four
In a large skillet, heat the oil over medium high heat. Gently place crab cakes in the oil. Crab cakes are ready when brown on both sides. Drain on a wire rack set over paper towels. Serve with Dill Sauce: Stir together ¼ Cup Light Mayonnaise, ¼ Cup Sour Cream, 2 TB chopped Dill, 1 TB Whole Grain Mustard. Season with salt and pepper.

Tasty Wine Tip
Four Vines Naked Chardonnay *Santa Barbara County, California*
Total Wine about $12.00

Here's a crowd favorite: a crisp, fresh and appealing Chardonnay to pair with the crab cakes. This one is substantial enough to hold up to the rich seafood, but also lean and not oaky because of 100% stainless steel fermentation. You'll enjoy the taste of crisp apples with citrus and a medium long finish.

Terrific Tilapia Tacos

Who doesn't love fish tacos? They have taken the nation by a storm! Now you can make them at home as easily as ordering them when you go out.

 *Pescetarian*

Tilapia

1-2 LBs Tilapia Filets, cut in strips
¼ Cup Panko Bread Crumbs
2 TB Cornmeal
½ Tsp Smoked Paprika
4 Cups shredded Napa Cabbage
½ Cup shredded Carrots
¼ Cup thinly sliced Green Onions
2 TB chopped Cilantro
    Juice and Zest of 2 Limes
2 TB Extra Virgin Olive Oil
Sea Salt and Pepper to taste
6 -12 Corn Tortillas, warm
1 Recipe Tilapia Taco Sauce
Lime and Avocado for Garnish

Step One

Preheat the ovne to 350°F. Bread the Tilapia by placing the panko, cornmeal and paprika in a plastic zippy bag. Add the tilapia slices a few at a time and shake to coat well. Place the slices on a sheet tray and cook for 5 - 8 minutes or until the fish is flaky and white.

Step Two

While the fish is cooking, add the cabbage, carrots, onions cilantro, juice, zest and oil to a bowl. Toss, taste for salt and pepper.

Step Three

Place the slaw and a few slices of tilapia in each taco. Top with a healthy dollop of sauce.

 Taste and Savor TV: Chopping Herbs

Kitchen Smidgen

It's probably no surprise to you that Tilapia is one of the top ten fish types consumed in the U.S. Tilapia are native to Africa, but now most are farmed in Latin America, Asia and the U.S. The statement: "it doesn't taste fishy" makes Tilapia the perfect candidate for almost any recipe calling for mild, white and flaky fish.

get creative

Tilapia Taco Sauce

½ Cup Light Mayonnaise, 1 TB Lime Juice, 2 TB chopped
Pickled Jalapenos, 1 TB chopped Cilantro, Sea Salt
and Pepper to taste. Place the the ingredients in a bowl
and stir to combine.

Tasty Wine Tip

Burgans Albarino  *Rias Baixas, Spain*
Kroger, Total Wine about $15.00

You couldn't pick a better wine for fish tacos than a refreshing Spanish Albarino. The grape
and the wine are the same. Its aroma will remind you of limes, and it tastes crisp and light,
with a lots of citrus and good acidity combined with just a taste of honey.

Salmon Tikka
with Mint Chutney

Summer or winter, this is one of my go-to salmon dishes. Spicy yet not hot, the fish has the perfect mix of flavors to contrast with the fresh minty salsa.

 *Pescetarian*

The Salmon

4 Skinless Salmon Filets

2 Tsp Sea Salt

2 TB Fresh Lemon Juice

½ Cup Yogurt

1 TB White Vinegar

1 TB Garam Marsala

1 TB Ground Cumin

½ Tsp Cayenne Pepper

1 TB grated Garlic

½ Tsp Black Pepper

Mint Chutney

2 Garlic Cloves

8 -10 Mint Leaves and Stems

½ Cup chopped Cilantro

1 Jalapeño, Ribs and Seeds removed

1 Large Mango, peeled and pitted

1 Tsp Ground Cumin

6 Whole Grape Tomatoes

Sea Salt to taste

Place all the ingredients in a food processor and finely chop.

 Taste and Savor TV: Grating Garlic and Ginger, Using Chiles, Chopping Herbs, Cutting a Mango

Kitchen Smidgen

The word "Tikka" means everything from "woodpecker" in Finnish to the mark Hindu men may wear on their foreheads. In our case it refers to the marinade used in the preparation of salmon - made with a mixture of aromatic spices and yogurt.

get creative

*You can call it Salsa, Relish or Chutney – but it's the same
idea the world over. Sweet and sour, chutneys are usually made
with fruit and sugar. Try serving this mint chutney with corn
chips, it's delicious!*

Step One
Cut the fish filets in cubes or long slices. Sprinkle with the salt and juice and set aside for 30 minutes.

Step Two
Place the remaining ingredients together in a zippy bag. Place the fish in the bag and massage to coat the pieces. Set aside to marinate for an hour.

Step Three
After taking the fish from the zippy bag, remove any excess marinade by patting with paper towels. If desired, place on skewers. Cook (on grill pan, grill or under the broiler) for 2 - 4 minutes on each side over medium high heat. Garnish with Cilantro if desired and serve with Mint Chutney.

Tasty Wine Tip
Kunde Estate Winery Viognier  *Sonoma California*
Total Wine about $18.00

Far from Viognier's traditional home in France, this silky smooth charmer is a great match for the spicy South Indian Salmon Tikka. Kunde Estate Viognier (vee-ohn-yay) is as aromatic as a Gewürztraminer and has a good medium mouth feel like a Chardonnay. You'll enjoy honeysuckle and peaches when you smell and drink it.

Orange Shrimp
over Citrus Couscous

In the middle of January when its especially dark and gloomy outside, this citrusy entrée hits all the right notes. The ginger and fresh orange flavor are a welcome change from the usual heavy fare during the cold months – try it and shake up dinner tonight!

 *Pescetarian*

½ Cup White Wine

½ Cup Orange Juice

1 TB grated Garlic

1 TB chopped Dill

1 LB Large Shrimp, shelled and deveined

Salt and Black Pepper to taste

2 Cups Whole Wheat Couscous

2 TBs Unsalted Butter

1½ Cups grated Romano Cheese

Zest of 2 Oranges

2 TB Olive Oil

3 TB chopped Red Onion

2 TB grated Fresh Ginger

Zest and Juice from 1 Orange

2 TB chopped Dill, plus more for garnish

Kitchen Smidgen

If you have been segmenting, (cutting between each section), your oranges or grapefruits before serving them, Stop! The thin white membrane on the inside of the citrus is full of flavonoids – antioxidants that are compounds that protect cells against damaging effects. Just slice and serve for big flavor and lots of good health benefits.

get creative

Couscous can be made of barley, corn or semolina, but whole wheat couscous tastes nutty and toasty. Tiny grains of pasta make a quick and easy dish that acts like a sponge, soaking up any delicious flavors you add.

Step One
Place the wine, juice, garlic, dill and shrimp in a zippy bag, seal and set in the fridge for at least an hour – up to 4 hours.

Step Two
Remove the shrimp from the fridge, discard the marinade and sprinkle with salt and pepper. Set aside while you prepare the couscous as the package directs. Add the butter, romano and zest to the cooked couscous and stir to combine. Cover and set aside.

Step Three
Heat a large sauté pan over medium high heat and add the oil. When warm, add the onions and ginger and sauté for 2 minutes. Add the shrimp and sauté for an additional 3 - 4 minutes or until just pink. Remove from the heat and add in the zest, juice and dill. Serve the couscous topped with the shrimp and garnished with more dill.

Taste and Savor TV: Grating Garlic and Ginger, Chopping Herbs

Tasty Wine Tip
Zenato Pinot Grigio Venato, Italy
Total Wine about $14.00

This Pinot Grigio is from Sergio and Carla Zenato, winemakers committed to making affordable wines with exceptional quality – and they succeed! Zesty and refreshing, Zenato Pinot Grigio is bright and clean tasting with aromas of citrus and tropical fruits.

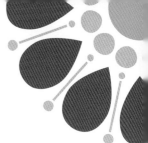

Fruit and Herb Stuffed Red Peppers

These are definitely NOT your mother's stuffed peppers! Whether it's hot and steamy outside or cold and blustery, here's a perfect weeknight meal. If you eat veggie all the time, or just occasionally, it's a power packed dinner that even meat lovers will enjoy. Filled with fat, ripe, red tomatoes, herbs and fruits – all it needs is a quick green salad and some crusty bread to make a meal.

8 Red, Orange or Yellow Peppers

¼ Cup + 2 TB Olive Oil

2 Large Red Onions, thinly sliced

1" Piece of Ginger, grated

¼ Tsp Allspice

2 Cinnamon Sticks

½ Cup Basmati Rice, rinsed

6 peeled, seeded and chopped Tomatoes

8 Ounces Dried Apricots, chopped

2 Ounces Dates, coarsely chopped

1 TB Lemon Juice

2/3 Cup Hot Water

½ Cup chopped Parsley

¼ Cup chopped each Cilantro and Mint

¼ Cup Pine Nuts, toasted

¾ Cup sliced Almonds, toasted

2 TB Golden Raisins

Sea Salt and Black Pepper to taste

2 TB toasted Fresh Breadcrumbs
    tossed with ½ Tsp Olive Oil

Vegetarian

Fruit and Herb Stuffed Red Peppers

Step One
Preheat the oven to 350°F. Cut the tops off the peppers and remove the seeds. Set aside.

Step Two
To create the stuffing, heat the ¼ cup oil in a large pan and sauté the onion until golden. Add the ginger and spices and cook and stir for 1-2 minutes until aromatic. Add the rice and sauté for 1-2 minutes until coated with the oil. Add $2/3$ of the tomatoes, fruits, juice and water. Let it simmer for 10 minutes until most of the liquid has been absorbed. Remove from the heat, remove the cinnamon and add the next 6 ingredients.

Step Three
Place the shrimp on the grill until just opaque - about 2-3 minutes.

Step Four
To create the sauce, toss the remaining tomatoes and the 2 TB of oil together and place on the top of the peppers and pan. Cook for 45 minutes, basting the peppers with sauce from the bottom of the pan.

Step Four
To create the sauce, toss the remaining tomatoes and the 2 TB of oil together and place on the top of the peppers and pan. Cook for 45 minutes, basting the peppers with sauce from the bottom of the pan.

Step Five
Turn the oven up to 425°F. Scatter the breadcrumbs on top, and bake until the crumbs are golden.

 Taste and Savor TV:
Using a Mandoline, Grating Garlic and Ginger, Chopping Herbs, Toasting Nuts

Kitchen Smidgen

Easiest way to grate ginger? Break out your microplane or the small side of a tower grater.

get creative

Dried Fruits like dates, raisins and apricots are a great way to add sweetness and interest to a savory dish. Try adding some dried cranberries or mango to prepared brown rice or couscous - Delicious!

Tasty Wine Tip

Hahn Estates Cabernet  *Central Coast California*
Total Wine about $16.00

You may be familiar with the Cabernet Franc grape from it's home in France, but this Californian is a pleasing pair with both veggies and meat. Full of spicy dried fruit taste, it's a good summertime light red that's smooth, subtle and low in tannins.

Spiced Chickpea Curry

My friends at Cancer Wellness are all big advocates of this flavorful, easy and a super make-ahead curry. The reason is simple; it tastes great and is packed with good-for-you spices. The beautiful yellow color from the turmeric indicates just how powerful the antioxidants are in the delicious dish. Add some purchased whole wheat naan bread, and you've got dinner and lunch for tomorrow, too!

Vegetarian

2 TB Olive Oil
1 Tsp Turmeric
1 Tsp Cumin
½ Tsp Freshly Cracked Black Pepper
1 Tsp Garam Masala
¼ Tsp Cayenne Pepper
1 Tsp Ground Coriander
1 Red Onion, chopped
1 TB grated Ginger
4 Cloves Garlic, grated
1 Cup Water
1 (14.5 oz) Can Fire Roasted Tomatoes
2 Cans Chickpeas, drained and rinsed
1 Tsp Sea Salt, plus more to taste
1 Cup Light Coconut Milk
To garnish: thinly sliced Red Onions,
Chopped Fresh Mint and chopped Tomatoes

Kitchen Smidgen

Basmati Brown Rice Pilaf is a perfect accompaniment to the delicious curry - and couldn't be easier. Cook the Basmati as the package directs. As soon as the rice is cooked, stir in a bag of defrosted frozen green peas and 2 TB chopped cilantro. Replace the lid on the rice. Let sit for 10 minutes and serve.

get creative

Loaded with the anti-oxidant Curcumin, Turmeric is not only a spice with beautiful color and flavor but super healthy. You can increase the bioavailability of the antioxidants by heating the turmeric with black pepper and olive oil. Try using turmeric in any recipe where you sauté aromatic veggies like onions and garlic – you will increase the good-for-you factor as well as the taste!

Step One

Heat the oil in a large saucepan over medium-high heat. Add the spices and stir until fragrant. Add in the onion, and ginger, and cook until the onion is wilted. Stir in the garlic, the can of tomatoes, water, and chickpeas. Bring to a boil, reduce the heat to low, cover and simmer until chickpeas are soft, about 20 - 30 minutes. Taste and season with salt.

Step Two

After the chickpeas are softened, use a potato masher and mash them a bit. Don't mash them all, just about a quarter of the chickpeas. Add the coconut milk and cook and stir for another 10 minutes or so - this will thicken the sauce. Serve, with Basmati Brown Rice and topped with garnishes.

 *Taste and Savor TV:*

Chopping Ginger and Garlic, Chopping Onions, Chopping Herbs

Tasty Wine Tip

D'Arenberg Viognier/Marsanne. The Hermit Crab Adelaide Hills, Australia   Total Wine about $12.00

Tannic wines taste bitter when paired with curries; they strip wine's fruit flavor, leaving it too astringent. This Viognier/Marsanne blend with the funny name is not tannic - and is a great pair with any curry or seafood. Made mostly with the Viognier grape, it is chock full of peach aromas and lots of citrus-melon taste.

Flavorful Ratatouille Pasta

I love making this pasta on the fly. Whatever veggies are lying tired in the bottom of the frig drawer go in to roast. Perfect fast dinner, this pasta topping gives you loads of antioxidants plus fiber and tastes great, too!

 *Vegetarian*

1 Zucchini, in 1-inch cubes

1 Yellow Squash, in 1-inch cubes

1 Fennel Bulb, in 1 by 2 inch strips

1 Small Eggplant, in 1-inch cubes

10 Cherry Tomatoes, halved

2 TB Olive Oil

Sea Salt and Black Pepper

1 Cup minced Red Onions

1 TB minced Garlic

4 Cups chopped, seeded Ripe Roma Tomatoes

1 TB Thyme Leaves

1 TB Balsamic Vinegar

½ Cup Capers

2 Roasted Red Peppers, chopped

Cooked Whole Wheat Penne Pasta

 Taste and Savor TV: Chopping Onions, Chopping Herbs, Roasting Peppers

Kitchen Smidgen

Don't save them just for salad - Red Onions add color and flavor to any cooked dish. Although they lose some of their red color when sautéed, they still maintain a sweet mild flavor, and can be substituted for yellow onions in almost any recipe.

get creative

Fennel is a hardy perennial herb with leafy fronds. It tastes like a cross between celery and cabbage with a slight hint of licorice. For a delicious change, try substituting chopped fennel the next time a recipe calls for celery.

Step One
Preheat the oven to 425 degrees. In a large bowl; toss the zucchini, squash, fennel, eggplant and cherry tomatoes with 1 TB of the oil, salt and black pepper. Spread on a sheet pan in a single layer and roast for about 30 minutes, until soft and very browned.

Step Two
To prepare the tomato sauce, heat the remaining TB of oil in a large nonstick skillet over medium heat. Add the onion, and season with salt and pepper to taste. Cook for about 5 minutes, until the onion is translucent. Add the garlic, chopped tomatoes, and the thyme leaves, stirring to combine. Cook over medium heat for about 20 minutes. Remove from the heat and add the capers and the balsamic vinegar.

Step Three
Add the vegetables and peppers to the tomato sauce. Adjust the seasoning as necessary. Top cooked pasta with the sauce.

Tasty Wine Tip
Domaine de la Curniere Vacqueyras  *Vacqueyras, Southern Rhone, France*
Total Wine about $17.00

Vacqueyras, (Vah-keh-rahss), is both the area and the name of this dark berry tasting wine. Made from a blend of Rhone grapes, with Grenache taking the lead, Vacqueras wines are typically fruit forward and juicy with a medium body and a nice finish. Domaine de la Curniere is no exception!

Rustic Italian
Spinach Cannelloni

I love having friends over at the spur of the minute. "Come on over for a kitchen dinner!" is one of my favorite ways to invite others for a casual meal. I created this recipe as one that can go from freezer to table without a lot of supervision. This Cannelloni is a real winner, easy to fix, warm and comforting, and a crowd pleaser whether you are serving adults or children. If you haven't experimented with whole wheat pasta before, try it with this recipe. Just follow the directions on the box, and it will add a nutty and toasty flavor to the Cannelloni.

Vegetarian

4 Boxes Frozen chopped Spinach
1 Pkg Lasagna Noodles
1 TB Olive Oil
½ Cup minced Yellow Onions
1 TB minced Garlic
2 Tsp Italian Seasoning
1½ Tsp Sea Salt
15 Oz Ricotta Cheese
1 Large Egg
⅛ Tsp Freshly grated Nutmeg
½ Tsp Black Pepper
1½ Cups grated Pecorino Romano
¼ Cup minced Fresh Parsley
3 Cups Tomato Sauce (Your Choice)
2 Cups shredded Mozzarella

Step One
Defrost and then ensure the spinach is dry by placing it in a clean linen kitchen towel, (or paper towels), and wringing it out.

Step Two
Cook the lasagna noodles per the package directions. Drain the noodles well and lay them out flat.

Step Three
In a skillet over medium heat, add the onion and cook until soft in the olive oil. Add the garlic, Italian Seasoning and ½ Tsp salt. Cook for 1 minute.

 Taste and Savor TV: Chopping Onions, Grating Ginger and Garlic

Kitchen Smidgen

Ricotta is made from the whey drained from cow's milk cheese like mozzarella.
Ricotta's name means "cooked again" and refers to the method of production.

get creative

Add Nutmeg to more than just baked goods. Nutmeg adds a sweet and spicy touch to vegetables - try grating a little fresh nutmeg in any dish containing green leafy vegetables. Delicious!

Step Four

Place the Ricotta cheese, egg, nutmeg, pepper and remaining 1 Tsp of salt in a bowl. Add ½ cup of the Romano and the minced parsley to the bowl. Add the spinach.

Step Five

Turn the oven to 350°F. Spread about 1 cup of the tomato sauce in the bottom of a 9x12 baking dish. Cut each about ¼ cup of spinach filling onto each noodle and roll up to enclose the filling. Arrange the cannelloni in the baking pan, seam side down.

Step Six

Cover the cannelloni with the remaining tomato sauce and sprinkle the rest of the Romano, as well as the Mozzarella on top. Bake the cannelloni until the sauce bubbles up under the melted cheese, or about 45 minutes.

Tasty Wine Tip

Il Valore Sangiovese 🍇 *Puglia, Italy*
Trader Joes about $4.00

How about a pleasant red, that goes with not only tomato-saucy Italian dishes but is good for quaffing on it's own? Try Il Valore Sangiovese. The Sangiovese grape is the main component of Chianti and produces a ruby colored wine with aromas of strawberry and cherries. You'll be surprised by Il Valore Sangiovese. - especially for the price.

Wonderful Penne Puttanesca

Interested in a savory, rich, fast, but good for you pasta? You are in the right spot! Pasta Puttanesca hails from Sicily, and is attributed to the "working girls" of the region. They were interested in a quick bite between customers, so they surveyed their pantry and created this yummy meal. Most if not all the ingredients you will already have on hand, so it's easy to whip up on a weeknight. As a bonus it's super fast so you can have it on table quickly. Don't like spicy food? Just reduce the amount of red pepper flakes – you can take them down to a pinch – but make sure you include them. They add just that right amount of "ummm" to the dish.

Vegetarian

1 TB Canola Oil
1 Yellow Onion, finely chopped
3 Cloves Garlic, minced
1 Tsp Red Pepper Flakes
4 Cups Canned Chopped Tomatoes
½ Cup Dry Red Wine
1½ TB Balsamic Vinegar
1 Tsp Sugar
1 Tsp Each Sea Salt and Pepper
6 Anchovy Fillets, chopped
3 TB Capers
1 Cup Kalamata Olives, chopped
1 Box Whole Wheat Penne
2 TB chopped Parsley
Grated Pecorino Romano to serve

Step One

Heat the oil in a saucepan and sauté the onion and red pepper flakes over medium high heat for 3-5 minutes, or until soft. Add the garlic and sauté for 1 minute, then the tomatoes and wine. Bring to a boil, reduce the heat and simmer for 10 minutes.

Step Two

Season with the balsamic vinegar, sugar, salt and pepper. Add the anchovies, capers and olives and simmer for an additional 3-5 minutes, or until warm. While the puttanesca is simmering, cook the pasta according to package directions.

Step Three

Toss the pasta with the pan of puttanesca sauce. Serve garnished with parsley and cheese.

Kitchen Smidgen

Anchovies are a dividing food - either you love them or you hate them! But even if you are not an anchovy fan, try cooking them, as in this recipe. When the anchovies are heated they simply dissolve, leaving a luscious salty flavor.

get creative

Penne (Pen-A) is short wide tube of Italian pasta. The name comes from the Latin word for quill or feather. It's a perfect pasta for "saucy" dishes because of it's hollow interior which catches all the goodness. It's available in a smooth or a ridged version. Try it with any thick sauce - hot or cold, just make sure not to overcook it.

Tasty Wine Tip

Caldora Montepulciano D'abruzzo   *Abruzzi, Italy*
Total Wine about $11.00

Here's a versatile everyday red that shines when enjoyed with tomato sauces. It's made primarily with the Montepulciano (Mont-ta-pull-chi-on-oh) grape. It has a beautiful deep ruby color, with medium body, nice acidity and light tannins. You'll smell plums and cherries and taste berries and vanilla when you drink it.

Summer Mediterranean Pasta

*In 2008, I had the pleasure of serving as the chef at a local farmer's market.
Each week I used local produce as the inspiration for a dish. In August,
the warm weather, incredible tomatoes, squash and herbs made perfect
harmony for the creation of this Mediterranean pasta.*

 *Vegetarian*

2 Lbs Zucchini or Summer Squash, halved and sliced into ½" Pieces
1 TB Sea Salt
3 TB Extra Virgin Olive Oil
1 Cup finely chopped Onion
2 Garlic Cloves, grated
Zest and Juice of a Lemon
2 Cups quartered Grape Tomatoes
¼ Cup chopped Mint Leaves
1 TB Red Wine Vinegar
½ Cup chopped Calamata Olives
½ Cup Crumbled Feta Cheese
Chopped Mint and Oregano to garnish
1 Pkg Whole Wheat Pasta cooked and drained per box directions
Sea Salt and Fresh Black Pepper

Kitchen Smidgen

When cooking with summer squash, always salt and allow them to drain off
any excess liquid. This will ensure your finished dish is not watery.

get creative

Calamata, (Kalamata) olives are from Greece, and named for the city around which the olives are grown. They are especially fruity tasting with a meaty texture. Their unique flavor is enhanced by the vinegar marinade that they are often soaked in. Calamatas are sold packed in oil or vinegar.

Step One
Place the squash in a colander and sprinkle with salt. Set aside for at least 30 minutes. Remove from colander and pat dry.

Step Two
In a large skillet, over high heat, cook the squash in 1 TB oil until brown around the edges, about 7 minutes. Remove from the pan.

Step Three
Add the onion and sauté in 1 TB oil until soft, about 3 minutes. Add the garlic, lemon zest and juice, 1 TB oil, tomatoes, mint, vinegar and olives to the pan and cook until warm. Add the squash back in and taste for salt and pepper. Serve over the whole wheat pasta, sprinkled with feta and garnished with oregano and mint.

 *Taste and Savor TV:* Chopping Herbs

Tasty Wine Tip
Amano Primitivo 🍇 *Puglia, Italy*
Total Wine about $11.00

Blackberries, Cherries, Fruit Jam and just a hint of Licorice are all evident in this perfect-for-pasta wine. This one's easy to remember because the grape and the wine name are the same. The name Primitivo is from a word meaning "Early Riser" because it is one of the first grapes to ripen each year. The briny olives and feta cheese make the zing of acidity in Amano Primitivo sing with flavor!

Pat's Quinoa with Roasted Red Peppers and Chickpeas

My sister has always been my best friend – in the kitchen and out. We have long shared memories of cooking together, laughing and enjoying a glass of wine. Quinoa is one of the delicious foods that she introduced me to a couple of years ago. She is a real master of seasoning and always manages to pull the best flavors out of any food. I think you will agree with me when you make this Quinoa dish.

 *Vegetarian*

1 15 oz Can Chickpeas, rinsed
3 TB Fresh Lemon Juice
3 TB Extra Virgin Olive Oil, divided
3 Large Garlic Cloves, grated
1 TB Cumin seeds
2 Tsp Turmeric, divided
2 Tsp Smoked Sweet Paprika, divided
2 Cups Water
1 Cup Quinoa, rinsed and drained
1 Tsp Sea Salt
2 Tsp Ground Cumin
1 Roasted Red Pepper, Julienned
4 Green Onions, thinly sliced
¼ Cup chopped Fresh Parsley
Sea Salt and Black Pepper

Kitchen Smidgen

To roast Red Peppers, preheat a grill, grill pan or broiler. Grill or broil until browned on all sides. Place in a zippy bag and let rest until cool. While still in the bag, rub the black skin off the roasted red pepper.

get creative

Try serving Quinoa (Keen-wah), tonight. Revered by the Incas as the "mother grain" it is actually a seed from the Goosefoot plant. Sold in the U.S. only since the mid-eighties, it has a mild nutty flavor that is a great background for strong bold flavors - like smoked paprika, lemon juice and garlic. Try substituting Quinoa for Couscous in your recipes!

Step One
Combine chickpeas and lemon juice. Add 2 TB olive oil, stir in the garlic. Let the mixture marinate for at least 15 minutes.

Step Two
Heat 1 TB olive oil in a medium saucepan. Add cumin seeds, 1 Tsp turmeric, 1 Tsp paprika and stir until fragrant – 2-3 minutes. Add 2 cups of water, quinoa and salt. Bring to a boil and then reduce heat to medium-low. Cover and simmer until all water is absorbed – about 15 minutes.

Step Three
Stir in the ground cumin, the remaining turmeric, and paprika to the quinoa. Add the roasted red pepper, green onions, parsley and the chickpea mixture. Taste for salt and pepper and serve.

 Taste and Savor TV: Grating Garlic and Ginger

Tasty Wine Tip
Falesco Vitiano *Umbria, Italy*
Cost Plus World Market about $10.00

How about a young red with a big nose of fruit and spice aromas to match with the smoky "garlic-y" flavor of your Quinoa? This darling-of-the-winecritics wine is created with equal parts of Merlot, Cabernet and Sangiovese. You'll enjoy jammy dark fruit flavors with balanced acidity and nice tannins.

Luscious Lentil Burgers

I created these delicious sliders for an "alternative" burger class and they are so delish – they are eaten at my house at least once a month. Fast to cook and a perfect make ahead freezer meal, these will slide right in your loved one's lunchbox often. Even if you are not a veggie burger fan, try this one!

 *Vegetarian*

3 Cups Lentils

4 Large Eggs

2 Tsp Sea Salt

¼ Cup minced Red Onion

¼ Cup grated Carrots

2 TB minced Fresh Cilantro

1 TB Tomato Paste

1 Cup Panko Breadcrumbs

½ Tsp Freshly Ground Black Pepper

1 TB Garam Masala or Curry Powder

2 TB Canola Oil

Step One

Preheat the oven to 350°F. Place the lentils into a pan and cover with 6 cups of cold water. Add onion, fresh parsley, or other herbs. Bring the water to a boil and simmer gently for about 20 – 40 minutes or until the lentils are tender. Drain and remove the herbs.

Put the lentils, eggs and salt in a food processor and using the pulse feature – process until combined.

Step Two

Combine the onion, carrots, cilantro, tomato paste, breadcrumbs, spices and processed lentils in a bowl. Let stand for 30 minutes to allow the panko to absorb some of the liquid. Form into patties and place into the fridge for about 30 minutes to firm them up.

Step Three

Sauté the burgers in the oil until browned on both sides - about 5 minutes, turning only once. Place them in the preheated oven for an additional 5 minutes to heat through. Serve in Pita Pockets with Caramelized Red Onions and Chutney Mayonnaise.

Kitchen Smidgen

Caramelized Red Onions are SO delicious - and easy to make. Slice 2 red onions and add to a TB of hot oil in a sauté pan. Over medium heat, cook and stir until the onions are soft. Give them a good sprinkle of salt and pepper and add ½ cup red wine, chicken or veg stock. Cook and stir until the liquid is evaporated and the onions are meltingly tender.

get creative

Mayonnaise is a great carrier of taste. Use a ¼ cup of Light Mayo and add ingredients like bottled chutney, wasabi or capers to brighten up flavors in any sandwich.

 Taste and Savor TV: Chopping Onions

Tasty Wine Tip

Cambria Pinot Noir Julia's Vineyard   *Santa Mari Valley, California*
Total Wine about $18.00

A light and refreshing Pinot Noir is a great find. If you like cherry, strawberry and raspberry flavors, this is the wine for you. It's a versatile summer sipper from the central coast of California - perfect with alternative burgers as well as the traditional beef slider right off the grill.

Italian Root Vegetable Risotto

Risotto does not have to be hard to make or "bad" for you. I hope this easy and delicious recipe will inspire you to try your hand with it. It's lighter and filled with luscious veggies, including one you may not have used often – parsnips. So grab your favorite wooden spoon, and start stirring.

 *Vegetarian*

5 - 6 Cups Vegetable Stock
1 TB Unsalted Butter
1 TB Olive Oil
1 Medium Red Onion, minced
3 Carrots, grated
3 Parsnips, grated
1½ Cups Arborio Rice
½ Cup Dry White Wine
½ Cup grated Parmesan
Salt and Pepper to taste
Fresh Herbs for garnish

Step One
Pour the stock in a saucepan and bring it to a simmer.

Step Two
Combine the butter, oil, and minced onion in a large heavy skillet. Cook over medium heat for about 5 minutes, until the onion is translucent and soft.

Kitchen Smidgen

Risotto means, "little rice" in Italian. Risotto differs from other rice dishes in that the cooking vessel is never covered, and liquid is added bit by bit, stirring often, until the rice is cooked but still a little al dente.

get creative

Wondering about that funny looking white carrot in the produce department? It's a parsnip. A relative of the carrot, it tastes slightly sweet but starchy, and it's a great addition to any meal where a root veggie is desired. Try substituting parsnips for carrots in almost any recipe!

Step Three

Add the carrots and parsnips and cook until softened about 5 minutes. Add the rice and stir, continuing to cook until slightly golden, about 5 minutes more.

Step Four

Once the rice is toasted, add white wine slowly, stirring with a wooden spoon. When the white wine is absorbed, start adding the warm vegetable stock, ½ cup at a time, stirring often, and adding more stock when previous batch is almost absorbed. Continue adding the stock as the rice absorbs the liquid. Add the liquid a little at a time while stirring constantly in order to release the rice's starch. You want the grains of rice to be firm - not mushy or chalky. (This whole process should take about 20 - 25 minutes). Remove from the stove, stir in the grated cheese, taste for salt and pepper and garnish with fresh herbs.

Taste and Savor TV: Chopping Onions

Tasty Wine Tip

Sokol Blosser Evolution Number 9   *Williamette Valley, Oregon*
Total Wine about $15.00

Sokol Blosser is a pioneering winery in Oregon that makes some delicious Pinot Noirs, as well as the fun Evolution series - perfect to pair with a veggie risotto. Evolution Number 9 is a unique blend of 9 different grapes that bring apple and pear aromas and tastes to the glass combined with bright acidity and a smooth finish.

Three Cheese Pasta with Broccoli

My friend and colleague Shayna tells a wonderful story about her son Andrew. A precocious 4 year old, he has not eaten a lot of packaged food. (Yes, Shayna is a dietician.) When served the ubiquitous orange mac and cheese at a party, he asked the hostess, "What is this?" Here's a scrumptious alternative to the blue box that no one will have to ask, "What is this?" And, since it's lighter and filled with good-for-you veggies, you can enjoy it without any guilt. It also freezes great, just pop it out and cover it with aluminum foil – cook in a 350°F oven until brown and bubbly.

 *Vegetarian*

1 LB Box Whole Wheat Penne

1 8 Oz Bag Broccoli Florets

¼ Cup Whole Wheat Flour

3 Cups Skim Milk

8 Oz shredded Fontina Cheese

2 OZ Light Cream Cheese

¼ Cup grated Parmesan Cheese

1 Tsp Sea Salt

½ Tsp Freshly Ground Black Pepper

¼ Tsp Cayenne Pepper

Butter Flavored Non Stick Spray

½ Cup Whole Wheat Panko Bread Crumbs

½ Cup grated Parmesan Cheese

Kitchen Smidgen

Panko may sound exotic, but they are just the Japanese version of breadcrumbs. Typically made without the crusts, they are crispier and crunchier than regular breadcrumbs. Ian's is my favorite brand, because it is sold in a whole wheat version.

get creative

Cayenne pepper takes its name from its place of origin - the Cayenne region of French Guiana. It may seem unusual to add chili pepper to a cheese and pasta dish, but by adding just a little, it brings out the flavors of the mild cheese and makes it "cheesier". Try adding a pinch to your favorite cheese dish, and see if it doesn't make it taste even better!

Step One
Cook the pasta according to package directions, drain and return to the pot to keep warm. Steam or microwave the broccoli until just crisp-tender, add to the pasta in the pot.

Step Two
Preheat the oven to 350°F. Combine the flour and milk in a large saucepan over medium heat. Cook 10 minutes or until it begins to thicken, stirring constantly. Remove from the heat and add the cheeses, stirring until smooth. Add the salt, pepper, cayenne, cooked pasta and broccoli, stirring well. Spoon pasta mixture into an oval or rectangular baking dish that has been coated with non-stick spray.

Step Three
Sprinkle the panko and the parmesan over the top of the casserole, then spray with the butter flavored spray. Place in the oven and cook for 25 – 30 minutes or until brown and bubbly.

Tasty Wine Tip
Cape Mentelle Sauvignon Blanc/Semillon  *Margaret River, Western Australia*
Total Wine about $16.00

Are you familiar with Semillon? The Semillon grape hails from France where it can be found in Bordeaux wines from Sautérnes to Graves. This wine is a blend of smooth Semillon with tart Sauvignon Blanc, making it the perfect partner to accompany the rich and creamy pasta. You'll find it a beautiful light straw color and smell and taste tart citrus with very dry acidity.

Roasted Poblanos and Cheese with Best Ever Guacamole

This guacamole is so good, so easy and so true to the delicious taste of avocados that it's worth building an entire meal around its simple goodness. Accompany it with some cheese-topped poblanos and warm corn tortillas and call it dinner.

 *Vegetarian*

½ Cup Fresh Salsa OR ½ Cup Light Sour Cream
Sea Salt
8 Roasted Poblano Peppers
2 Cups grated Light Jalapeno
Cheddar Cheese

Step One
Prepare an oven proof casserole with non stick spray. Spread the bottom of the dish with either the salsa or the sour cream. If you are using the sour cream, lightly salt it.

Step Two
Place the poblanos on top of the salsa or sour cream and top with the cheese. Bake in a 350°F oven for 20 - 30 minutes or until the cheese is melted. To roast the poblanos, heat the grill or a grill pan on high. Grill for 3 - 5 minutes per side or until blackened. Place in a zippy bag until cool enough to handle. Remove stems, seeds and skin and tear into strips.

Kitchen Smidgen
Poblano is the name for a resident of Pueblo, Mexico AND a Pepper. Enjoy Chile Rellenos? You've probably eaten Poblanos. They have a delicious mild taste and a shiny dark green color. Because of their waxy exterior, they are most often used roasted and peeled. When dried, poblanos are called anchos.

get creative

Corn Tortillas are the perfect partner for this dinner. The easiest way to warm them is to carefully seperate each one in the stack. Place the stack in a barely damp kitchen towel and microwave for about 30 seconds.

Best Ever Guacamole

4 Ripe Haas Avocados
¼ Cup finely chopped, (peeled and seeded) Tomatoes,
1 TB minced Red Onion
1 finely chopped Jalapeno
¼ Cup chopped Cilantro
Sea Salt to taste
1 Cup grated Light Cheddar Cheese

Halve, peel and pit the avocados and mash with the tomatoes, onion, jalapeno and cilantro. Salt to taste and spread on a large platter. Sprinkle with the cheese.

Taste and Savor TV:
Peeling and Chopping Tomatoes, Chopping Onions,Chopping Herbs

Tasty Wine Tip

Villa Maria Riesling *New Zealand*
Total Wine about $12.00

Rich, creamy guacamole and cheese topped peppers call for a light, crisp and easy drinking sip. This Riesling from the much-lauded New Zealand winery, Villa Maria, will not disappoint. You'll smell lemon and lime aromas and savor fresh lime and other citrus fruit flavors.

sides and salads

Crispy, Crunchy, Cool or Warm and Comforting – Sides and Salads are not only a favorite way to cook, but a way of life as well! In our house, we have salads at least twice a week. Not only are the recipes in this chapter super, leftovers from the last chapter often find their way into our weeknight salads. Sides usually mean we are heading to a dinner with others, or having a piece of simple, (but delicious), fish or chicken from the grill. The recipes in this chapter are quick, easy, luscious and perfect for busy lifestyles.

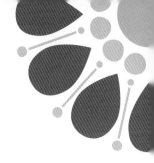

Crisp Citrus
Shrimp Salad

Most of us enjoy salads year round, but it's during the dog days of summer when all I can think of is getting in and out of the kitchen fast. I think you'll like the ease and convenience of this salad using bagged broccoli slaw as much as I do. And if you don't have shrimp handy – it works like a dream with pork tenderloin or chicken.

¼ Cup Lemon Juice

¼ Cup Frozen Orange Juice

3 TB Low Sodium Soy Sauce

2 TB Honey

1 Clove Garlic, grated

2 LBs Large peeled Shrimp

2 Cups halved Grape Tomatoes

¼ Cup chopped Cilantro

1 (15 OZ) Can Black Beans, well rinsed and drained

4 Ears Fresh Corn, Kernels cut from the cob

2 chopped, Roasted Red Peppers

1 Bag Broccoli Slaw

Zest of 1 Lemon and 1 Orange

2 TB Each Lemon and Orange Juice

2 – 4 TB Extra Virgin Olive Oil

½ Tsp Ground Cumin

½ Tsp Smoked Paprika

Sea Salt and Black Pepper to taste

Chopped Cilantro for Garnish

Pescetarian

Crisp Citrus Shrimp Salad

Step One
Combine the lemon juice, orange juice concentrate, soy sauce, honey, and garlic in a zippy bag. Add the shrimp, seal bag, and toss shrimp in bag to coat well. Marinate for up to 1 hour.

Step Two
In a large bowl, combine the tomatoes, cilantro, black beans, corn, peppers and slaw and toss.

Step Three
Whisk the zests, juices, oil, cumin, paprika together in a small bowl, or shake in a jar. Taste for salt and pepper. Pour the dressing over tomato mixture and toss. Set aside while you grill the shrimp.

Step Four
Remove the shrimp from bag and discard marinade. Place the shrimp on a clean well-oiled grill or grill pan and grill 2-3 minutes or until shrimp are done. Let the shrimp cool slightly, then toss with the salad and garnish with chopped cilantro. 16-20 per LB shrimp.

 Taste and Savor TV: Roasting Peppers, Chopping Herbs

Kitchen Smidgen
Did you know the terms used to describe shrimp size—small, medium, large—mean different things in different locales? A better way to buy shrimp is by the numbers. If the label says "20-28" that means there are 20 to 28 shrimp per pound.

get creative

There are hundreds of shrimp species available from striped to yellow to white, but all turn a beautiful pink when cooked. Next time you are in the market for shrimp, try a different kind – you may be surprised to learn you like it better.

Tasty Wine Tip

Avelada Vinho Verde 🍇 *Portugal*
Cost Plus World Market about $10.00

There's no better summer delight than a chilled bottle of Vinho Verde and a shrimp salad. You'll enjoy its crisp and fruity taste along with an aroma of oranges, limes and peaches. Plus, it's low alcohol level allows enjoyment of this light wine without becoming lightheaded!.

Grilled Salmon Salad with Peaches and Almonds

I call this type of recipe, a "cheater" recipe because you are using one ingredient, or a group of ingredients like the vinaigrette for two uses. In this easy recipe, you'll use the vinaigrette for both the salmon marinade and the salad. AND, you'll have a little left over to dress a salad tomorrow night, too!

 *Pescetarian*

¼ Cup Extra Virgin Olive Oil
¼ Cup Balsamic Vinegar
2 TB Lime Juice
Zest of 1 Lime
2 TB Honey
1 Tsp Sea Salt
½ Tsp Pepper
4 Skinless Salmon Fillets (4-6 oz)
½ Cup toasted Almonds, chopped
3 Cups Mixed Greens
3 Cups Baby Spinach
2 Peaches, peeled and chopped

 Taste and Savor TV: Toasting Nuts, Peeling Tomatoes

Kitchen Smidgen

Did you know that salmon fisheries in Alaska haul in more than 700 million pounds of the flavorful fish in a year? If you a wild salmon fan, you'll love the website http://www.salmonnation.com Not only is there lots of interesting information about this versatile fish, the recipes are delicious.

get creative

Top a scoop of frozen vanilla yogurt with these mouthwatering Vanilla Poached Peaches. To 2½ Cups Water add ½ Cup each Fresh Lemon Juice and Orange Juice, ¼ Cup Peach Brandy or Peach Nectar, ½ Cup Honey (or ¼ cup Agave Syrup) and 1 Vanilla Bean, split and seeds scraped out. Bring to a boil and add 4 Peaches and return to a boil. Reduce the heat and simmer for 20 minutes until peaches are tender. Remove the peaches. Boil the syrup for 20 minutes until reduced by half. Peel, pit and slice the peaches and serve with the syrup.

Step One

Whisk the olive oil, balsamic vinegar, lime juice, zest. honey, salt and pepper in a bowl until well blended. (Or shake the ingredients in a jar.) Baste each fillet with a Tsp of the vinaigrette. Grill salmon on oiled hot grill, (or grill pan), turning once during cooking, about 4-5 minutes or until desired doneness.

Step Two

Toss the salad greens with some of the vinaigrette. Place the salad greens on 4 plates or in large flat bowls. Top with the peaches, warm salmon and almonds. To toast raw almonds, spread them out on a sheet tray. Slide them in a 350°F oven for 8 minutes - set your timer! Check the nuts, if they are not done, set your timer for 2 more minutes. At 10 minutes, remove the nuts and set aside to cool.

Tasty Wine Tip

Santa Ema Reserve Merlot   Maipe Valley, Chile
Cost Plus World Market, Total Wine about $12.00

Hello Merlot! This incredible Chilean value proves that red is perfect with salmon right off the grill. You'll find ripe dark cherries and plums in the aroma and a lovely full mouth feel accented with more of those cherries, plus juicy, jammy blue and black berries.

Crisp and Crunchy
Asian Salad

This is a salad that you can easily personalize. Got leftover Turkey, Duck, Pork or Beef? Perfect for the salad. If you're starting from scratch, try the Asian Vinaigrette as a marinade as well as a dressing!

 *Flexitarian*

1 Bag Baby Greens
1 Bag Baby Spinach
4 Scallions, thinly sliced
1 Can Water Chestnuts, drained and rinsed well
2 Cups shredded Carrots
1 Cup thinly sliced Snow Peas, blanched
½ Cup sliced toasted Almonds
1 - 2 Cups sliced Holiday Leftovers: Turkey, Duck, Pork or Beef, even Tofu
1 Recipe Asian Vinaigrette
Toasted Sesame Seeds for garnish

Asian Vinaigrette
¼ Cup Rice Vinegar
2 TBs Light Soy Sauce
2 TBs Lime Juice
Zest of 1 Lime
1 TB Honey (or ½ TB Agave Syrup)
1 TB Natural Peanut Butter
1 Garlic Clove, grated or minced
2 TB Dark (Roasted) Sesame Oil
½ Cup Peanut Oil (Roasted Peanut Oil if Possible)
¼ Cup Canola or Vegetable Oil
Salt and Pepper to taste

Toss the first 7 ingredients together in a large bowl, dress with vinaigrette and top with sesame seeds.

Combine all the ingredients in a jar or bowl. Shake or whisk till well combined.

Kitchen Smidgen

Water Chestnuts are not nuts at all! An aquatic vegetable that grows in marshes, it brings a crisp snappy crunch to Chinese food. Lately, fresh water chestnuts have been appearing in grocery stores, although they are most often found in a can. Expect to see fresh ones more often - traditionally grown in China, semitropical areas in California and Florida are now cultivating them. Water chestnuts are low in fat and full of fiber and vitamin B.

get creative

Just like toasted nuts, roasted nut oils add more than oil to a recipe - they add lots of concentrated flavor. Try substituting some or all of the oil in your salad dressing with a nut oil and discover how delicious your dressing can be.

 *Taste and Savor TV:*
Toasting Nuts and Grating Garlic and Ginger

Tasty Wine Tip

Yalumba Y Series Viognier   *South Australia*
Kroger, Publix about $12.00

Clear gold, bright and fruity, you'll find this Viognier, (vee-yohn-yay), is a good match for Far Eastern flavors. After enjoying stone fruits like apricot and peach on the nose, you'll find it tastes of tropical fruit balanced off with a good bit of acidity. Enjoy this affordable Aussie with any Asian-inspired meal.

Roasted Sweet Potatoes with Curried Chicken Salad

This recipe is a must try! An innovative way to serve amp up the veggies in a chicken salad – the sweet potatoes add lots of flavor, too.

 *Flexitarian*

2 Large Sweet Potatoes, peeled and cut into slices about ½" thick
1 TB Olive Oil
Sea Salt and Black Pepper to taste
2 Large Boneless Skinless Chicken Breasts, Roasted and chopped
½ Cup chopped Green Onions –Green Parts Only
¼ Cup Light Mayonnaise
¼ Cup Greek Yogurt
1 Tsp Garam Masala (or Curry Powder or Smoked Paprika)
½ Tsp Cumin
¼ Tsp Cayenne Pepper (or to taste)
Zest and Juice of a Lemon
¼ Cup sliced Almonds, toasted
½ Cup Dried Fruit, (Golden Raisins, Cranberries, Apricots), chopped
¼ Cup chopped Parsley

 Taste and Savor TV: Toasting Nuts

Kitchen Smidgen

When you are looking for color, crunch and just a bit of onion flavor - nothing beats green onion tops.

get creative

Both sweet potatoes and white potatoes contain a variety of nutrients, but the sweet potato wins in many categories. They are loaded with antioxidants and fiber, too – about twice as much as an ordinary baking potato. Sweet potatoes are a delicious addition to your kitchen anytime of the year. Try switching to sweet potatoes in some of your recipes to ramp up the taste and the nutrition.

Step One

Preheat the oven to 425°F. Toss the sweet potatoes with the oil. Arrange them in a single layer on a baking sheet and salt and pepper to taste. Bake until tender and lightly browned, about 20 minutes. Remove from the oven and set aside.

Step Two

While the sweet potatoes are cooking, make the chicken salad by combining the chicken, green onions, mayo, yogurt, garam masala, cumin, cayenne, lemon juice and zest. Season to taste with salt and pepper.

Step Three

Place several sweet potato slices on a plate and top with a dollop of chicken salad on each one. Garnish with the almonds, dried fruit and parsley.

Tasty Wine Tip

Heath Southern Sisters Riesling   *Clare Valley, Australia*
Cost Plus World Market about $15.00

A great sea of Riesling has been grown in Australia for years. But most was poor quality, cheap and consumed locally. Now, all has changed - this dry, complex white from Clare Valley is a good expression of today's Australian offerings. Crisp, with good acidity – you'll smell peaches and apricots and enjoy lemon and minerals as you drink it.

Chicken and Pomegranate Grape Salad

I love pomegranates in any form, whole, juice and seeds. This refreshing fruit salad uses an ingredient that you may not have seen before, Pomegranate Molasses. Check out the entry for it in the kitchen staples in the back of the book, I think you decide it needs to be one of your kitchen staples, too!

Flexitarian

1 TB Lemon Juice

1 Cup Non Fat Greek Yogurt, plus
    more as desired

2 TB Pomegranate Molasses

1 Head of Fennel, chopped

6 Green Onions,
    Green Parts Only, sliced

1 Cup chopped toasted Pecans

¼ Cup chopped Italian Parsley

2 Cups Grapes, cut in half

2 Cooked Chicken Breasts,
    Cut in 1" Pieces

Sea Salt and Black Pepper to taste

1 Large Bag Baby Spinach Leaves
    tossed with Champagne Vinegar
    and Sea Salt and Pepper to taste.

Pomegranate Seeds for garnish

Step One

In a large bowl, mix the lemon juice, yogurt and pomegranate molasses together. Toss the fennel, onions, pecans, parsley, grapes and chicken into the bowl with the yogurt mixture. Season to taste with salt and pepper. Serve on the dressed spinach, garnished with pomegranate seeds.

Kitchen Smidgen

You may want to consider buying organically grown grapes. The Shoppers Guide to Pesticides at www.foodnews.org has a list of the "Clean 15" and the "Dirty Dozen" that can help you in your decisions about what fruits and veggies to buy conventionally grown or organic. Of course, local fruits and vegetables are the best, and luckily we are almost at peak growing season!

get creative

When cooking your chicken, make it special by adding a sprinkle of herbs or spices. Some good choices for this recipe include curry powder or garam masala, smoked paprika or even a dusting of Italian seasoning.

Taste and Savor TV:
Chopping Onions

Tasty Wine Tip
La Vieille Ferme Rose   *Côtes du Ventoux, France*
Cost Plus World Market about $12.00

Travel just east of the southern tip of France's Cote du Rhone and you'll find the home of this watermelon, floral and rich dark strawberry charmer. It's a blend of Cinsault, Grenache and Syrah grapes fermented in stainless steel for a bright, dry and very drinkable quaffer. Why so pretty and pink? The grape skins were left in contact with the grape juice for 24 hours.

Mediterranean Chicken Salad

Here's a chicken salad with unusual flavors that will hold well in the fridge for a couple of days. So you could have it for lunch or dinner – and then snack on it later. I hope you find it as appetizing as I do. Without mayo it's a great picnic partner as well

 *Flexitarian*

2 Cooked Chicken Breasts, chopped
1 Cucumber peeled, seeded, diced
12 Kalamata Olives, pitted and chopped
1 Roasted Red Pepper, chopped
1 Pint Grape Tomatoes, quartered and drained
¼ Cup Red Onion, minced
4 Oz Feta Cheese, Crumbled
1 Recipe Simple Vinaigrette
Salt and Pepper to taste
To Serve: Pita Pockets, Home
Made Pita Chips or shredded Romaine

Kitchen Smidgen

It's pretty obvious why the grape tomato earned it's name. But did you know that you can't grow more tomatoes from the seeds? (You'd have to order special seeds.) That's because it is a hybrid – bred specially for it's thick skin and flavor, which is noticeably sweeter than a Roma or cherry tomato. Some bars in Asia offer customers bowls of grape tomatoes instead of peanuts!

get creative

Pomegranate Molasses is simply reduced Pomegranate Juice. You can make your own by boiling down pure pomegranate juice to about $\frac{1}{8}$ of its original volume - or buy it in an international market or Whole Foods. Make sure to look for the bottle with 100% Pomegranate on the label. Try using it anytime a recipe calls for honey or agave nectar - it's sweet and delicious.

Place the ingredients together in a bowl and toss well. When using vegetables with lots of liquid, like tomatoes, cucumbers or squash, chop the veggies and place them in a colander over a bowl. Salt lightly and let drain for at least 30 minutes before using them. Your finished dish will not turn out watery.

Simple Vinaigrette
¼ Cup Extra Virgin Olive Oil
2-3 TB Balsamic (or Your Choice) Vinegar
1 Tsp Dijon Mustard
½ Tsp Pomegranate Molasses
Salt and Pepper to taste
Add the ingredients to a jar with the other ingredients and shake.

Tasty Wine Tip
Brancott Pinot Grigio  *South Island, New Zealand*
Publix about $16.00

No — it's not a Sauvignon Blanc from New Zealand, but a Pinot Grigio that pairs perfectly with Mediterranean Chicken Salad. You'll notice the color is very pale yellow color, with an aroma of citrus, zest and pear. It has a lush taste of tropical fruit, peaches and pears with a refreshing acidity and a crisp aftertaste.

Retro Crunchy Romaine
Salad with Green
Goddess Dressing

Happy 70s! Here's a flashback to an earlier era. Crisp and crunchy, dressed with a herby blend of veggies and creamy goodness, this salad is a real hit with friends and family. Make sure to use the leftover dressing, (you'll have some), as a dip for fresh veggies. The dressing will stay good in the fridge for about a week.

Flexitarian

1 Large Clove Garlic

4 Anchovies

1 Cup Lightly Packed Parsley Stems and Leaves

½ Cup Lightly Packed Fresh Tarragon Leaves

3 Coarsely chopped Green Onions

½ Cup Light Mayonnaise

½ Cup Light Sour Cream

1 Cup No Fat Plain Greek Yogurt

¼ Cup Tarragon Vinegar

3 TB Light Buttermilk

Sea Salt and Black Pepper to taste

6 Strips Lean Turkey Bacon

2 (1") Slices of Whole Grain Bread cut in 1" cubes

2 Heads Romaine Lettuce, chopped

1 Head of Red Radicchio, sliced

2 Cups of Packed Spinach Leaves

1 Pint Grape Tomatoes, quartered

Kitchen Smidgen

Because we are using a food processor, no need to chop the herbs first! Just bunch them up, and lightly pack them into a measuring cup.

get creative

When preparing bacon, make sure to rest it on a wire rack after cooking. Placing it on paper towels allows it to sit in the fat, instead of draining it away. Use this tip when you sauté or fry any food - to ensure crispy, light results.

Step One
Place the garlic and anchovies in the food processor or blender and mix well. Add the next 8 ingredients, (through the buttermilk) to the bowl and process again until creamy. Adjust the seasoning with salt and pepper.

Step Two
In a skillet over medium heat, cook the bacon until crisp. Remove and place on wire rack over paper towels to drain. When cool, crumble the bacon. To make the croutons, add the bread to the skillet and cook and stir until bread cubes are golden brown.

Step Three
Toss the lettuce, radicchio and spinach together in a large salad bowl. Toss with the dressing, (beginning with ¼ and tossing just to dress – not drench) and divide between 4 - 8 plates or bowls. Top with crumbled turkey bacon, tomatoes and croutons.

Tasty Wine Tip
Veramonte Sauvignon Blanc  *Casablanca Valley, Chile*
Cost Plus World Market about $13.00

Just because this wine has a screw top, doesn't mean the contents aren't racy and vibrant - full of juicy grapefruit and citrus flavors. Carefully controlled fermentation using all stainless steel creates conditions that encourage freshness and lively aromas that are delicious with a crisp and crunchy green salad.

Fresh Tomato Basil Dressing

Salad classes are some of my favorites to teach. I am often inspired by the fresh, crunchy goodness of greens - so I developed this salad dressing to use up lots and lots of wonderful basil. Of course it's best in the middle of summer when there are so many tomatoes you can't keep up with them – but try it in the winter too, when you need a spicy, herby lift to the day.

 *Flexitarian*

Makes about 1½ Cups
1 Large Ripe Tomato, seeded
¼ Cup Fresh Parsley, chopped
2 TBs Fresh Basil, chopped
¼ Cup Balsamic Vinegar
½ Cup Light Mayonnaise
1 TB Dijon Mustard
2 Garlic Cloves, grated
2 TB Extra Virgin Olive Oil
Sea Salt and Black Pepper

Step One
In a food processor, puree all the ingredients except for the Oil, Salt and Pepper.

Step Two
With the processor running, add the Oil slowly. Taste for Salt and Pepper.

Make it an Italian Tomato Salad:
2 Heads Romaine, chopped
1 Cup shredded Skim Mozzarella
¼ grated Fresh Parmesan
1 Can Garbanzo Beans (Chickpeas), rinsed well and drained
1 Roasted Red Pepper, Cut in Thin Strips
1 Cup chopped Tomatoes
¼ Cup Capers, rinsed
2 Cups Fresh Croutons

Toss all the ingredients together - drizzle with Fresh Tomato Basil Dressing, toss again and serve

 Taste and Savor TV: Chopping Herbs

Kitchen Smidgen

Seeding Tomatoes is easy. Cut a large ripe tomato in half - and then in fourths. Use your thumb to run between each section of the tomato and remove the seeds.

get creative

Make Toasts to serve with Cheese, or Fresh Croutons to toss with a Salad. Take a good Baguette, and cut into ½" slices for Toasts - or 1" cubes for Croutons. Scatter on a sheet tray and place in a 350°F oven. Set your timer for 5 minutes, check and turn over. Set your timer for 3 minutes longer, check and remove if lightly toasted. If not, set the timer for 2 minutes more - now they are ready to enjoy.

Tasty Wine Tip

Chateau Ste. Michelle Pinot Gris   *Columbia Valley, WA*
Valley Publix about $13.00

Two words best describe this wine: Refreshing Crispness. Imagine biting into crunchy apple or perfectly ripe pear - finished with a nice lift from lemony acidity. Now you know what to expect from this food friendly quaffer. Try it with any of your favorite summer salad combinations. It sings with shrimp and chicken too! Made from Pinot Gris grapes and a touch of Viognier, it's a fun change from Italian Pinot Grigio.

Spring Strawberry Jam Salad

Gorgeous strawberries, sweet strawberry jam and gorgeous fresh greens make this salad appetizing in Technicolor! Chicken or pork star in this salad equally well.

Vegetarian

The Dressing and Marinade

¼ Cup Strawberry Jam
¼ Cup Balsamic Vinegar
1 Tsp Dijon Mustard
3 TB Extra Virgin Olive Oil
½ Tsp each Sea Salt and Black Pepper
1 Large Chicken Breast

The Salad

8 Cups Spring Greens - Baby Spinach, Arugula or other Lettuces
1 Cup shredded Red Cabbage
1 Cup shredded Carrots
2 Cups sliced Strawberries
4 Oz Goat Cheese, Crumbled
¼ thinly sliced Green Onions
½ Cup toasted chopped Almonds

Kitchen Smidgen

When strawberries are in season, you can make your own quick and easy refrigerator jam. Just take 2 cups of hulled strawberries - mash them with ½ cup of sugar or honey and 4 Tsp fruit pectin. Put them in the microwave for 4 minutes on high, or until it comes to a rolling boil. Microwave on medium for another 5 minutes or until it starts to get thick. (It will thicken more as it gets cool.) Store in your fridge for up to a week.

get creative

Make a little "jam butter" to spread on toasted bread and serve it with your salad. Add ¼ cup of strawberry jam to a stick of softened unsalted butter. Place in a ramekin and serve with a toasted whole wheat baguette.

Step One

To make the dressing, add the jam, vinegar, mustard and oil to a jar and shake well. Season with the Sea Salt and pepper. Add ½ of the dressing to a zippy bag with the chicken breast. Place in the fridge for at least 4 hours or overnight. Remove the chicken from the bag, pat dry and cook on the grill or grillpan. When done, remove from the grill and let sit for 5 -10 minutes. Slice the chicken breast on the bias.

Step Two

To make the salad, toss together the salad ingredients. Beginning with half of the remaining dressing, toss the salad, adding more if necessary. Top the salad with the sliced chicken breast.

Tasty Wine Tip

Domaine/Maison Joseph Drouhin  *Beaujolis, France*
Total Wine about $11.00

You'll enjoy every drop of this light red wine made from the Gamay grape in the southern region of Burgundy. Strawberries and raspberries will greet you in the aroma, and sweetness and just a hint of spice makes this a perfect choice for cool spring sipping.

Avocado and Mango Lime Salad

I have to admit that this is one of my favorite salads. Juicy gold mangoes, fat red tomatoes and creamy green avocados - this African inspired salad is one of the most colorful around. Make sure to use only the ripest most beautiful fruit for this succulent salad. It makes a delicious centerpiece for your table AND your meal. If you are looking for a fast and fun appetizer, try skewering the mango and avocado with shrimp and watch the smiles!

Vegetarian

1 TB Lime Juice

1 TB Lime Zest

½ Tsp Dijon Mustard

¼ Cup toasted Nut Oil (Almond, Hazelnut, Walnut, etc.)

1 Jalapeno, Seeds and Ribs removed, minced

½ Cup chopped Parsley

Sea Salt and Freshly Cracked Black Pepper

2 Ripe Mangoes

2 Roma Tomatoes

2 Ripe Avocados

2 TB toasted chopped Almonds

Chopped Parsley for garnish

Kitchen Smidgen

Did you know you can buy jalepenos that are either green or red? The red jalepenos are just like red bell peppers that are riper and sweeter than green bell peppers. When using red jalepenos add 2 to the recipe to get the required heat and zippy flavor.

get creative

If you are looking for a reliable tomato until the good ones come in - try a Roma. It has less moisture and fewer seeds, and is a good substitute until you can score the really big red juicy orbs.

Step One

To make the dressing, whisk the lime juice, zest, mustard and oil together in a medium sized bowl. Add in the jalapeno and the parsley. Taste for salt and pepper and set aside.

Step Two

Peel, pit and slice the mangoes. Toss them in the dressing and set aside for 30 minutes to 1 hour.

Step Three

Chop the Roma tomatoes and place in a colander over a bowl. Salt lightly and allow to drain.

Step Four

Peel, pit and slice the avocados. Fan them out on one side of a plate. Remove the mango from the dressing (reserve the dressing) and do the same on the other side of the plate. Place the tomatoes over the middle of the fruit, and drizzle the dressing over all. Garnish with the parsley and the almonds.

Tasty Wine Tip

Mulderbosch Cabernet Sauvignon Rose  *Stellenbosch, South Africa*
Cost Plus World Market about $11.00

For those of you who are still rose-phobic this is a perfect wine to make the switch! Mulderbosch, (from Stellenbosch) is bone dry with a beautiful pink color, aromas and tastes of strawberries, cherries and just a touch of minerality.

Modern Day Bean Salad and Avocado Vinaigrette

Hope you can pack some of this bean salad and avocado dip for your next potluck, tailgate or neighborhood party. They are both delicious, and filled with color and flavor. And the good news is that both can be made ahead of time - the bean salad benefits from a stay in the fridge, and the avocado vinaigrette dip doesn't turn brown because of the olive oil.

 *Vegetarian*

1 (15 oz) Can Chickpeas
1 (15 oz) Can Black Beans
1 (15 oz) Can Cannellini Beans
2 Roasted Red Peppers sliced
¼ Cup Extra Virgin Olive Oil
4 Ounces Asiago or Manchego Cheese, chopped in ½" cubes
1 TB Italian Seasoning
½ Cup Fennel, chopped finely
Juice of 1 Lemon
1 Cup chopped Green Onion
Sea Salt and Black Pepper to taste
Fresh Herbs for garnish

Rinse and drain the canned beans. Toss the next 7 ingredients together and season to taste with salt and pepper. Garnish with fresh green herbs.

Kitchen Smidgen

Taste is your biggest ally when creating simple recipes. Remember to taste as you go along - do you need more lemon juice? Another grind of pepper? Tasting is the big difference between ho-hum and flavorful food.

get creative

Cut 2 roasted red peppers into strips and place in a bowl. Drizzle with ¼ cup extra virgin olive oil and add one peeled, smashed garlic clove. Set aside to let the flavors develop for 30 minutes. Remove the garlic before using. (This makes a great grilled bread topper, too!)

Avocado Vinaigrette Dip

2 Large Haas Avocados, peeled and pitted

3 TB Fresh Lemon Juice

¼ Cup Extra Virgin Olive Oil

1 Tsp Dijon Mustard

1 Tsp grated Onion

¼ Tsp Crushed Red Pepper

Sea Salt and Black Pepper to taste

To prepare the dressing - place the ingredients in a food processor and blend until smooth. Season with salt and pepper.

Tasty Wine Tip

Cono Sur Pinot Noir *Chile*
Kroger, Publix about $10.00

Here's a fun bottle of affordable wine that both red and white lovers will enjoy with casual food. You'll get a real mouthful of luscious fruit forward flavors with this Pinot Noir: cherries, raspberries, plums and strawberries. Make sure to serve it cool, around 58°F or so. And to make it taste even better - Cono Sur winery is all about being green.

Crisp and Crunchy Apple Salad

I love fruit salads, don't you? They are such a wonderful combination of sweet and savory, crunchy, crispy, soft and sweet. I especially enjoy salads like this one in the winter, when we all may need a break from the wonderful soups and stews and heavier foods.

Vegetarian

¼ Cup Low-Fat Mayonnaise
¼ Cup Nonfat Plain Yogurt
2 TB Orange Juice
2 TB Orange Zest
½ Tsp Garam Masala
1 Cup grated Carrot
½ Cup diced Celery
1 Red Apple, Cored, diced
2 Green Apples, Cored, diced
1 Cup Red Seedless Grapes, halved
⅓ Cup chopped Dates
¼ Cup Pine Nuts, toasted

Step One

Mix mayonnaise, yogurt, orange juice, orange zest and Garam Masala in a small bowl to blend. (You can prepare this dressing up to a day ahead of time)

Step Two

Step Two In a bowl toss the grated carrot, diced celery, diced apples, halved grapes and chopped dates. Add dressing to salad and toss. Sprinkle salad with pine nuts and serve.

Kitchen Smidgen

Ever cooked with yogurt and found that your sauce or dressing was watery? Try either draining the yogurt - place it in a coffee filter, inside a sieve over a bowl - or try using Greek yogurt. It's thick and delicious and will not "weep" like regularly processed yogurt. It is made by straining the yogurt to remove the whey or liquid. It's widely available at your local grocery store.

get creative

To Make it Dinner: Poke lots of holes with a fork in a 1½ LB Pork Tenderloin. Place in a zippy bag and add ⅓ Cup Orange Juice, 1 TB Garam Masala, 1 Tsp Freshly Ground Black Pepper and ¼ Tsp Cayenne Pepper. Massage the bag to coat the meat. Marinate in the fridge for at least an hour, (or overnight). Remove from the fridge, pat dry and place in a 400°F oven. Cook for about 30 minutes or until instant reathermoeter is at 150°F. Remove from the oven and let it rest for 10 minutes. Slice and cut into strips. Place on top of the salad.

Tasty Wine Tip

Trimbach Gewurtraminer   *Alsace, France*
Total Wine about $19.00

If you are looking for a perfect match for the refreshing and tart Crunchy Apple Salad and Tenderloin, choose Gewurztraminer (Guh-vertz-trah-MEEN-er). Although having a German name, this "Gewurtz" is from the Alsace region in France. Trimbach is an internationally recognized vineyard that consistently produces wines with lovely aromas, good acidity and wonderful taste. This one is no exception!

163

Italian Panzanella Salad

Once you make this salad, it will become a firm feature on your weeknight rotation. The cheese used in this recipe, Ricotta Salada, is one that you may not have tried. It's a saltier firmer version that typical Ricotta. You can use it as a topper for pasta, too!

 *Vegetarian*

The Bread
4 ½" Slices Ciabatta (Crusty Italian) Bread
1 Clove Garlic, peeled
1 TB Extra Virgin Olive Oil

The Onion
¼ Cup Red Wine Vinegar
½ Small Red Onion, thinly sliced

The Salad Ingredients
2 LB Ripe Tomatoes, chopped in ½" Pieces
1 Cucumber, peeled, seeded and Cut into ½" Cubes
1 Red Pepper, Roasted, Cut into Thin Strips
1 Cup ½" cubes of Ricotta Salada
¼ Cup chopped Basil
¼ Cup chopped Mint
¼ Cup Capers, rinsed

Kitchen Smidgen

Capers are the unripened buds of a plant native to the Mediterranean. After the buds are harvested, they are dried in the sun, then pickled in vinegar or salt. Curing brings out their tangy flavor, similar to olives.

get creative

Ricotta Salada is an Italian Cheese that is a firmer, saltier version of Ricotta. Widely available in most grocery stores, it resembles feta in texture and is great for both crumbling and slicing - it's an Italian standard for fresh tomato salads, sauces and pastas.

 Taste and Savor TV: Using a Mandoline

The Dressing
1 Garlic Clove, grated
1 Tsp Sea Salt and Black Pepper
½ Cup Extra Virgin Olive Oil
Reserved Red Wine Vinegar

Step One
Brush the bread slices with the olive oil, and rub the garlic clove over the bread. Grill the bread over medium heat - or brown the bread under the broiler. Remove and cut into ½" cubes.

Step Two
Combine red wine vinegar with the sliced onions and set aside while you prepare the salad ingredients.

Step Three
Drain the red onions, and reserve the vinegar. Make the dressing by shaking all ingredients together in a jar. Toss the dressing with the salad ingredients, cheese and bread.

Tasty Wine Tip
Ruffino Orvieto Classico  *Umbria, Italy*
Total Wine about $8.00

Here's a super white to drink from summer through Fall. Orvieto is the classic Italian white wine: cool and clean, light and dry with a crisp green apple and melon taste. Made from Trebbiano, Verdello and a variety of other native grapes, it's best to drink young - and with the great price of Orvieto you can pair it with any light salad, pasta or fish and enjoy it often!

Fresh and Crunchy Summertime Picnic Pasta Salad

Do you get tired of thinking about what to bring for a picnic or potluck? Me too! I'm often looking for a good salad or side to carry along. Here's one that is colorful, easy to make, and a real crowd pleaser. This salad uses fresh corn - if it's fresh and local, no need to cook it - just cut it right off the cob and use it. It adds a delicious crunch to fresh salads.

Vegetarian

1 Cup Whole Wheat Pasta, cooked as package directs

1 Can (15 oz) Black Beans well rinsed and drained

4 Ears Fresh Corn, cut from the cob

1 Cup chopped Tomatoes

½ Cup sliced Green Onion

3 TB Extra Virgin Olive Oil

Zest of 1 Lime

¼ Cup Lime Juice

¼ Cup Julienned Basil

½ Cup chopped Mint

½ Tsp Chili Powder

1 grated Garlic Clove

Sea Salt and freshly cracked Black Pepper, to taste

Shredded Romaine and Baby Spinach

Avocado Slices

Kitchen Smidgen

Did you know that pasta cooked al dente is actually better for you? The word "Al Dente" comes from Italian and means "to the tooth or to the bite". Pasta that is cooked this way is midway between under-cooked, where pasta is still tough, and overcooked, where it lacks any texture and begins to fall apart. Pasta that is prepared al dente has a lower "glycemic index" which means that it doesn't send your blood sugar skyrocketing.

get creative

Don't make the common (and hot) mistake of confusing chile powder with chili pepper. While chile pepper is pure chilies in ground form, chili powder is a mix of chile powder, cumin, garlic and other ingredients like paprika and oregano. There are 100's of chili powder blends out there — try several different brands to find your favorite.

Step One
In large mixing bowl, mix pasta, beans, corn, tomato, onions, Toss to combine.

Step Two
Whisk together the oil, zest, lime juice, basil, mint, chili and garlic together in a small bowl. Toss with the pasta mixture and taste for salt and pepper. Scoop the pasta salad on top of the shredded romaine and spinach, garnishing with avocado slices.

Tasty Wine Tip
Spy Valley Sauvignon Blanc  *Marlborough, New Zealand*
Whole Foods about $15.00

This salad calls for a full bodied sauvignon blanc with loads of tropical flavors to balance the chili and fresh herb flavors of the zippy dressing. Spy Valley, a real kiwi winner with many wine gurus, is full of lush tropical flavors with a crisp lime-tangerine finish.

Toasted Almond and
Apricot Wild Rice

This is one of my favorite salads. The reason I like it so much is versatility. It's good warm or room temperature, as a side or the main course. For some reason nutty wild rice always reminds me of fall – even though this yummy salad is good year round.

 *Vegetarian*

The Salad
1 (14) Oz Can Chicken Broth
1 Cup Wild Rice, rinsed
1 Cup shredded Carrots
¾ Cup sliced Almonds, toasted
½ Cup Dried Apricots, chopped
¼ Cup chopped Green Onions
Sea Salt and Black Pepper

The Dressing
1 Garlic Clove, minced
½ Tsp Sea Salt
¼ Cup Extra Virgin Olive Oil
3 TB Balsamic Vinegar
1 Tsp Curry Powder
1 Tsp Dijon Mustard
Freshly Cracked Black Pepper

 Taste and Savor TV: Toasting Nuts

Kitchen Smidgen

Did you know that wild rice is not rice at all? It is a grain that is high in protein, the amino acid lysine and dietary fiber. And, it's low in fat. Most of the wild rice we use comes from Minnesota, California or Canada.

get creative

Want to treat guests to this delicious dish? You'll have dressing left over from the salad. Use it to marinate chicken breasts for at least 30 minutes, or up to overnight. Sprinkle the chicken with salt and pepper. Either sauté or grill the breasts, and you have a meal fit for company.

Step One
Combine the wild rice and chicken broth in a saucepan. Bring to a boil, cover and reduce the heat. Simmer for 45 minutes. Keep the pot covered and set aside for 1 hour.

Step Two
While the wild rice is cooking, make the dressing. Mash the garlic together with the Sea salt to make a paste. Add the garlic paste along with the remaining ingredients to a jar and shake. Season to taste with salt and pepper.

Step Three
When the rice is tender, add the carrots, almonds, apricots and green onions, toss gently. Add the dressing, a little at a time. Season to taste with salt and pepper.

Tasty Wine Tip
Rocca Felice Nebbiolo d'Alba  *Piedmont, Italy*
Total Wine about $16.00

You may be familiar with the grape Nebbiolo from its use in Barolo, the famous, (and expensive), robust Italian red wine. Now, you have a chance to taste the grape, in a younger and softer style of wine. In Italy, Nebbiolo is typically served with risotto, so this week's nutty and fruity wild rice salad makes a perfect match. Enjoy this dry full-bodied velvety red wine that tastes of cherries and blackberries!

Kale Coleslaw

If you never used uncooked kale before, here's your chance. It is delicious! By massaging thinly sliced, or julienned kale with salt, you are actually cooking it: making it soft and pliable. Sound incredible? Just try the recipe and you will become a believer, too.

Vegetarian

The Salad

15-20 Kale Leaves, (about one
    small bunch – de-stemmed)
1 Tsp Sea Salt
1 Large Tomato, chopped coarsely,
    (salt lightly and let drain in
    colander for a few minutes while
    shredding the carrots)
¼ Head of Napa Cabbage, shredded
3 Carrots, grated
Toasted Sesame Seeds for garnish

The Dressing

2 TB Extra Virgin Olive Oil
1 TB Freshly Squeezed Lemon Juice
½ Tsp Low Salt Soy Sauce
1 Tsp Agave Nectar or Honey
1 Clove Garlic, grated
1 Tsp Dijon Mustard
Salt and Pepper to taste

Step One

To chiffonade the kale, stack the leaves and roll them into cylinders. Cut ¼ slices off the cylinders – resulting in thin ribbons of kale. Place the kale into a salad bowl and massage a Tsp of salt into the kale. Set aside while you make the dressing.

Step Two

Add the dressing ingredients to a jar and shake well. Taste for salt and pepper - or more lemon juice.

Step Three

Add the tomato, cabbage and carrots to the bowl with the kale, toss with the dressing and garnish with the toasted sesame seeds.

Kitchen Smidgen

Agave nectar is made from the Agave plant. (More popularly known for its nectar with a kick, Tequila.) It is sweeter than honey but has fewer calories. Since it's composed of mainly fructose, Agave nectar has a lower glycemic load. You can substitute Agave in almost any recipe. Since it is sweeter, use ½ to ¾ of the amount of honey or sugar called for in the recipe.

get creative

Kale is a highly nutritious vegetable with powerful antioxidant properties - that tastes great. Try substituting kale for other green leafy vegetables for a healthy and delicious change.

Taste and Savor TV:
Toasting Nuts, Grating Garlic and Ginger

Tasty Wine Tip

Bogle Sauvignon Blanc — *Monterey and Russian River Valleys, California*
Publix, Kroger about $10.00

Wine Spectator featured the 2007 vintage of this orangy-lemon-limey refresher as a best buy. After trying it, you'll know why. It doesn't have the acidity of a New Zealand kiwi, but its zingy green and citrusy flavors paired with a refreshing clean finish make it a great casual dinner partner.

Red Pepper and Fresh Thyme Cornbread with Goat Cheese

Do you think about cornbread with dinner? Here in the South we often think cornbread first! Here's a wonderful and easy cornbread recipe that is just the ticket to side with a fresh green salad or delicious soup.

 *Vegetarian*

¾ Cup All Purpose Flour
¾ Cup Yellow Cornmeal
1 Tsp each Sea Salt and Black Pepper
1½ TB Sugar
1 TB Baking Powder
1 TB chopped Fresh Thyme
⅓ Cup minced Red Pepper
¾ Cup grated Parmesan
8 Oz Low Fat Buttermilk
2 Large Eggs
3 TB Extra Virgin Olive Oil
1 Log of Goat Cheese (Chèvre)
Extra Virgin Olive for Drizzling

Taste and Savor TV: Chopping Herbs

Kitchen Smidgen

Goat Cheese is made all over the world, and appears in a wide variety of forms, although most often in a soft, easily spread cheese. Because goat milk tends to be leaner than cow milk, goat cheese is too!

get creative

And make a Lemon Thyme Dressing for your salad. In a jar, squeeze the juice of a lemon, add an equal amount of extra virgin olive oil. Add 1 Tsp dijon mustard and 1 Tsp chopped thyme leaves. Taste for salt and pepper. Shake and serve!

Step One
Preheat the oven to 425°F. Grease a loaf pan with non stick spray.

Step Two
In a bowl, mix the flour, cornmeal, salt, pepper, sugar and baking powder. Add the thyme, pepper and parmesan and mix.

Step Three
In a second bowl, beat together the buttermilk, the eggs and oil. Mix into the dry ingredients.

Step Four
Pour the batter into the prepared pan and bake for 25 - 30 minutes, or until a skewer comes out clean. Leave to cool on a rack.

Step Five
When ready to serve, cut 8 thick slices from the loaf and place on a baking sheet. Turn your oven to broil, and cook until the edges are toasted. Cut 8 slices from a log of Goat Cheese. Flip the bread over, and place the goat cheese on top. Run the slices under the broiler again until the cheese is warm and melting. Drizzle with olive oil, pepper and serve with a green salad.

Tasty Wine Tip
Kim Crawford Sauvignon Blanc  *New Zealand*
Costco about $16.00

France's traditional pair with goat cheese is Sancerre wine, made from the Sauvignon Blanc grape. With this wine, we'll take that notion to the other side of the world. Kim Crawford Sauvignon Blanc brings the same kind of extremely aromatic, dry but full bodied taste. You'll enjoy the perfect balance of crisp citrus and herbs in contrast with the creamy, melting goat cheese and cornbread.

Roasted Ancho Potato Salad

I had the pleasure of working with a team from Ted's Montana Grill for a fundraiser. I was challenged to come up with a side for their Bison Sliders. Here's my crunchy-and-full-of-veggies Roasted Ancho Potato Salad that we served to over 200 guests. It's perfect with a burger or chicken right off the grill!

 *Vegetarian*

Ancho Dressing:

3 TB Orange Juice

2 Tsp Dijon Mustard

2 Tsp Ground Cumin

2 TB Orange Zest

1 TB Honey

½ Tsp Ancho Chile Powder

⅓ Cup Extra Virgin Olive Oil

Sea Salt and Black Pepper

In a jar, shake the orange juice, mustard, cumin, zest, honey, and chile powder together, add in the oil and taste for salt and pepper.

Roasted Potato Salad:

3 TB Dijon Mustard

2 TB Extra Virgin Olive Oil

1 TB Italian Seasoning

2 Garlic Cloves, minced

4 LB Red Potatoes, in eighths

12 oz Broccoli Spears,
   Lightly steamed

3 Roasted Red Peppers, in Strips

4 Carrots, shredded

3 oz Calamata Olives, chopped

⅛ Cup Cilantro, chopped

⅛ Cup Parsley, chopped

Sea Salt and Black Pepper

Kitchen Smidgen

Ancho Chiles are a dried, reddish brown, heart shaped and wrinkled pepper with a wonderful sweet hot flavor. (Almost fruity flavor.) If they are fresh they are called poblanos. Try experimenting with different kinds of chile powders - your food will develop lots of new zip!

get creative

Italian Seasoning is a blend made from a combination of marjoram, oregano, basil, savory, thyme and rosemary. Make your own by combining your favorite Italian spices.

Taste and Savor TV:
Roasting Peppers,
Chopping Herbs

Step One
Preheat oven to 425°F. In a bowl, whisk together mustard, oil, Italian seasoning, and garlic. Add potatoes and toss until coated.

Step Two
Spread potatoes in one layer on sheet pan. Roast 20 min. Lower heat to 350°F, roast, about 10 min. or until browned and cooked through. Cool.

Step Three
In large bowl, toss potatoes, broccoli, peppers, carrots, olives, cilantro, and parsley with the dressing until well coated. Season with salt and pepper.

Tasty Wine Tip
Guigal Cotes du Rhone   *Rhone, France*
Cost Plus World Market about $12.00

What's better with a grilled burger and potato salad than a juicy glass of red? This Cotes du Rhone is made by one of the most famous wineries in France. It's blend of Grenache, Syrah and Mouvedre that is packed with fruit and flavor. You'll taste lots of red berries and a little spice in this great grilling wine.

Napa Slaw with Cilantro Dressing and Black Baked Beans

These are easy sides to make ahead for a party – and quick enough for weeknights, too. Each delicious dish can easily make a full meal as well. For the salad, just add some grilled chicken. For the black baked beans, top brown rice with the baked beans – Instant Dinner!

Vegetarian

⅓ Cup Rice Vinegar

1 Tsp Agave Syrup

2 Tsp grated Ginger

3 TB Canola

1 – 2 Jalapeños, finely chopped

½ Tsp Sea Salt and Pepper
 + more to taste

1 Small Head Napa Cabbage
 (1½ lbs), cored and shredded

3 Carrots shredded

8 Green Onions, thinly sliced

½ Cup chopped Cilantro

Whisk together vinegar, agave, ginger, oil, chiles, salt and pepper. Add remaining ingredients and toss well. Let stand 10 minutes before serving.

Black Baked Beans

1 TB Olive Oil

1 TB Turmeric

1 Tsp Each Salt and Pepper

¼ LB Turkey Bacon, chopped

1 Cup diced Red Onion

2 Medium Carrots, grated

2 Garlic Cloves, grated

2 Jalapeños, seeded and chopped

1 Cup Light Chicken or Veg Broth

¼ Cup Light Brown Sugar

¼ Cup Light Ketchup

3 TB Molasses

1 TB Dijon Mustard

1 TB Apple Cider Vinegar

2 (15-oz) Cans Black Beans, drained
 and well-rinsed

¼ Cup chopped Cilantro

Kitchen Smidgen

When you buy turkey bacon, make sure to buy at least 65% lean. Otherwise you are getting just about the same fat and calories as regular bacon.

get creative

Tumeric's active ingredient, Curcumin, has anti-inflammatory properties. Cook with this delicious yellow spice to add a dose of antioxidants to any dish.

Step One

Preheat oven to 400°F. Heat the oil in a large skillet over medium-high. Add the next 7 ingredients and sauté about 10 minutes, or until the vegetables soften. Reduce the heat to low and add the broth, brown sugar, molasses, mustard, ketchup, cider vinegar. Stir until combined and add the beans.

Step Two

Spoon into a 9"x12" casserole dish. Bake, uncovered, 45 minutes, until the beans are hot and crusty. Garnish with cilantro.

 *Taste and Savor TV:*
Using Chiles,
Chopping Onions, Chopping Herbs

Tasty Wine Tip

Huber HUGO Gruner Veltliner *Austria*
Trader Joes around $12.00

This white wine from Austria is named and made with the same grape – Gruner Veltliner. (GROO-ner FELT-lih-ner) A light citrus aroma compliments the taste of lemon, vanilla and tropical fruit flavors well, resulting in a refreshing spring sipper. Great for a backyard BBQ or just by the glass!

Fresh Herb Tabbouleh

The inspiration for this recipe comes from my sister. I was talking to her about the wonderful tomatoes we have been enjoying this past summer. She mentioned Tabbouleh – and right away I made a big batch for dinner. If you haven't tried Tabbouleh before, you must! It's a traditional North African dish incorporating ripe tomatoes, fresh herbs and bulgur wheat.

*Vegetarian*

1 Cup Bulgur Wheat
1½ Cups Tomato Juice, Boiling
Juice of 2 Large Lemons
¼ Cup Extra Virgin Olive Oil
1 TB Sea Salt
1 Cup Green Onions, minced
1 Bunch Flat Leaf Parsley, chopped
1 Bunch Fresh Mint, chopped
1 Large Cucumber, (or 2 small) seeded and diced
2 Cups Tomatoes, seeded and diced

Step One

Place the bulgur in a large bowl and pour the boiling tomato juice over it. Set aside for at least an hour until the juice is absorbed and the bulgur is tender. If any juice remains, allow to drain through a colander.

Kitchen Smidgen

Bulgur Wheat is a pre-cooked wheat that is ready to eat with just a soak. It's nutritious and versatile with a nutty taste. Try using Bulgur in your favorite rice recipe.

get creative

Spiced Pita Chips are a perfect dipper for Tabbouleh! Cut 6 Pita pockets around the equator, and then into triangles. In a large bowl, mix ¼ cup each olive oil; lemon juice; ½ Tsp black pepper; ½ TB each cumin, curry powder, Sea salt, garlic powder, paprika and cayenne. Toss the Pitas with the spices, bake in a 400°F oven for 10-12 minutes or until crisp.

 Taste and Savor TV: Chopping Herbs

Step Two
When the bulgur is ready, add the remaining ingredients and toss. Check for salt and cover or refrigerate. Serve the Tabbouleh with...

Grilled Chicken Skewers:
Combine 1 Yellow Onion,

4 Cloves Garlic,

¼ Cup Fresh Lemon Juice

½ Tsp each, Paprika and Cayenne,

2 Tsp Sea Salt,

1 Tsp Pepper and

1 Cup Non Fat Plain Yogurt in a food processor and puree.

Add the chicken to a zippy bag, add the yogurt mix and marinade in the fridge overnight. Remove and pat dry. Load on skewers, and cook on an oiled grill, 5 minutes on each side.

Tasty Wine Tip
Villa Vitale Pinot Grigio   *North East Italy*
Cost Plus World Market about $8.00

Tart and Bright, this week's wine is a light, clean match to the fresh taste of Tabbouleh. Pinot Grigio is the Italian name for the French grape, Pinot Gris. The Villa Vitale brand is a private label wine from Cost Plus World Market. Private label wine can often be a great opportunity to try good wine at lower prices, as winemakers often use good surplus grapes or wine from other local vintners. You'll taste crisp citrus, melon and bright acidity from this easy drinking wine.

· desserts

I think that lunch or dinner should always finish on a sweet note. That doesn't always mean a formal dessert; most of the time a piece of fruit is the perfect ending. But, if you are looking for a special treat that tastes delicious but is just a little bit better for you, read on!

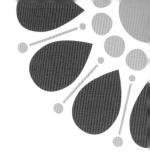

Gluten Free
Chocolate Chile Cake

I love flourless cakes – if you have a gluten free life style –
you probably do too! My friends Dennis, Angela and Sarah
all eat gluten free. This gives me the opportunity to learn
more about how I can make dishes they can enjoy as well as
everyone else. The chilies in this cake add just a certain "zing"
to the chocolate, and it uses toasted pecans instead of flour.
Unusual, distinctive and absolutely delicious are all accurate
descriptions for this recipe!

Non-Stick Spray
Sugar for the Pan + ¾ Cup Sugar
1½ Cups toasted Pecans
½ LB Bittersweet Chocolate, grated
2 Tsp Vanilla
1 Tsp Chocolate Chile Powder
¼ Tsp Cayenne
¼ Tsp Ground Cinnamon
8 Eggs, separated

Gluten Free
Chocolate Chile Cake

Step One
Preheat the oven to 350°F. Coat a 10" springform pan with nonstick spray, line the bottom with parchment paper and sprinkle the sugar over the bottom and sides of the pan, shaking out any excess.

Step Two
Combine the ¾ cup sugar and pecans in a food processor and grind until very fine. Transfer to a bowl. Stir in the chocolate, vanilla, chile, cayenne, cinnamon and yolks.

Step Three
Whip the egg whites until stiff peaks form.

Step Four
Fold the egg whites into the chocolate mixture, a third at a time. Pour the batter into the pan and pop in the oven. Cook 30 minutes - until the center is firm. Let cool completely before drizzling with:

Chocolate Chile Glaze
¾ Cup Cocoa Powder (*NOT dutch processed)
1 Tsp Cinnamon
2 Tsp **Chocolate Chile Powder
¼ Tsp Cayenne
4 TB Unsalted Butter, Softened
3 Cups Powdered Sugar
2 Cups Skim Milk
1 Tsp Vanilla Extract
Whisk together the cocoa powder, cinnamon, chile, and cayenne in a bowl. Beat the butter until creamy. Add the cocoa mixture and powdered sugar alternately with milk to the butter. Beat to drizzling consistency. Blend in the vanilla.

Kitchen Smidgen

Processing chocolate with alkali is known as the "Dutch" method". This causes the chocolate to lose a lot of the flavonoids and antioxidants we are looking for when we indulge in dark chocolate!

get creative

Chocolate Chile Powder is a blend of cocoa powder and chipotle peppers that packs a sweet heat - you can find it in your grocery store. If you want to create your own, combine 2 TB of Cocoa Powder and ¼ Tsp Chipotle Chile Powder together.

 Taste and Savor TV: Toasting Nuts

Tasty Wine Tip

Sofia Blanc de Blancs  *Monterey County, California*
Kroger about $15.00

This peach-colored charmer is a sparkling blend of pinot blanc, sauvignon blanc and muscat. Crisp and lively with a delicious aroma of lemon and honeysuckle, it's crisp taste makes it a refreshing, affordable and elegant pair with spicy chocolate cake.

Pumpkin Pecan Bars

These pumpkin, pecan and date filled treats are easy, quick and "eating better" snack bars - good with a glass of milk or a cup of coffee. You can whip up a batch of these delicious bars AND feel great about sharing.

Vegetarian

1 Cup Whole Wheat Pastry Flour

2 Cups Oats

1 Tsp Baking Soda

2 Tsp Cinnamon

1 Tsp Ground Allspice

½ Tsp Salt

1 Cup Canned Pumpkin

3 Eggs

1/2 Cup Canola Oil

2 Tsp Vanilla

1 Cup Dark Brown Sugar, packed

1 Cup chopped pitted Dates

1 Cup chopped toasted Pecans

Kitchen Smidgen

Did you know that Whole Wheat Pastry Flour has a higher starch content, and a lower gluten content than regular whole wheat flour? It's used in recipes like this one, where a tender result is desired. To maintain freshness, store your Whole Wheat Pastry Flour in the freezer. For more nutrition, try substituting up to ⅓ Whole Wheat Pastry Flour for White Flour in your baked good recipes.

get creative

Allspice is the dried berry of an evergreen tree that has a flavor of cinnamon, nutmeg and cloves. Traditionally it's used with pumpkin and winter squash dishes. Allspice is also great in tomato sauces - add a little bit to your barbeque sauce for extra zing!

 Taste and Savor TV: Toasting Nuts

Step One
Preheat the oven to 350°F. Coat a "9x12" baking pan with nonstick spray.

Step Two
In a bowl, combine the flour, oats, baking soda, cinnamon, allspice and salt.

Step Three
In a second bowl, mix the pumpkin, eggs, oil, vanilla and brown sugar together.

Step Four
Stir the pumpkin mixture into the flour mixture. Add in the dates and pecans.

Step Five
Spread the mixture in your prepared pan. Bake for 30 minutes, or until a skewer inserted in the top comes out clean. Cool completely before cutting.

Tasty Wine Tip
NV Taylor Fladgate Tawny Port, 10 Year Old *Portugal*
Total Wine about $28.00

Creamy and caramel Tawny Port is the perfect match for the rich autumn flavors in the Pumpkin Pecan Bars. The term "10 Year Old" indicates the average age of the wine used in making this port - older wines for complexity and younger wines which bring fresh flavors. Tawny Port is named for it's color, and can be aged in wood up to 40 years. It's a great fall after dinner beverage paired with any kind of fruit dessert.

Fresh Fig and Peach
Almond Crumble

During the heat of summer, there can't be a better dessert than this one. - I am very lucky to have so many friends with fig trees! When they are in season, we eat juicy figs in so many different ways. This recipe is a riff on a traditional crumble recipe - I think the toasted chopped almonds bring just the right nutty rich flavor to the sweet ripe summer fruit.

 *Vegetarian*

6 TB Unsalted Butter

⅓ Cup Dark Brown Sugar + 2 TB

1 ¼ Cup Whole Wheat Pastry Flour

6 TB very finely chopped toasted Almonds

1 LB Ripe Peaches, peeled and cut into ½" pieces

1½ LB Ripe Figs, Cut into ½" pieces

Zest and Juice of 1 Large Lime

½ Tsp Cinnamon

Vanilla Frozen Yogurt for serving

Kitchen Smidgen

Who knew? Although commonly referred to as a fruit, the fig fruit is actually the flower of the tree. Another good fig fact is that figs were one of the first plants cultivated. Fossilized figs have been found dating to about 9200 BC. And no wonder our ancestors loved figs – they are one of the highest plant sources of calcium and fiber. No matter how you eat them, in season or dried, they are fantastic!

get creative

One of the fastest ways to enjoy sweet ripe figs is to take off the stems and cut a deep cross in the top of each fig, put about 1 TB of creamy blue cheese (or whipped cream cheese) in each fig. Pack them closely together in a glass pie plate. Drizzle them with honey and place them in a 425°F oven until the cheese melts and the honey is warm. Enjoy them "melty and oozy" right out of the oven.

 Taste and Savor TV: Toasting Nuts

Step One
Spray a "9 x 12" casserole dish with nonstick spray. Preheat your oven to 350°F.

Step Two
Combine the butter and ⅓ cup brown sugar in a mixer. Beat until smooth. Add 1 cup of the flour and the almonds and beat until just combined - it should be crumbly.

Step Three
Place the peaches and figs in a bowl and toss with the zest and juice of the lime. Stir in the remaining ¼ cup flour, 2 TB brown sugar and the cinnamon.

Step Four
Place the peaches and figs mixture in the bottom of the prepared dish. Sprinkle the flour and almond mixture on top and bake for 30 - 40 minutes or until brown and bubbly. Serve warm topped with the vanilla frozen yogurt. No Peaches? Substitute any other Ripe Summer Fruit.

Tasty Wine Tip
NV Fonseca Vintage Character Port Bin 27  *Portugal*
Total Wine, Kroger about $16.00

This wine is deep dark and sweet with aromas of chocolate, candied fruit and cherries. It's dessert in a glass that perfectly complements the juicy rich flavors of the figs and peaches. If you've never enjoyed a glass of port after dinner this is a super introduction to the fortified wines of Portugal.

Fast Fresh French
Lemon Yogurt Cake

Lemony, Moist and Delicious, this recipe is a very traditional
sweet in France; most families have their own version. I learned
how to make it, (and enjoy eating it), during a cooking class in
Provence. Here's my twist on this fast and easy treat. It tastes
great for breakfast, lunch, tea or dinner.

Vegetarian

The Cake:
1½ Cups All-Purpose Flour
2 Tsp Baking Powder
2 Tsp Lemon Zest
½ Cup Nonfat Plain Yogurt
1 Cup Sugar
3 Large Eggs
½ Cup Canola Oil

The Glaze:
⅓ Cup Fresh Lemon Juice
¼ Cup Powdered Sugar

Kitchen Smidgen

A *Mandoline is the best tool for slicing thinly. Not only does it do a beautiful job on onions - it's perfect for this sweet citrus garnish. You don't have to buy a big professional stainless model - there are some great inexpensive plastic ones that pop right into the dishwasher!

get creative

A fun and eye-catching way to garnish citrus desserts is by slicing your citrus very thinly - about ⅛ " and add a little sugar. Stir well and set aside for at least 15 minutes to macerate. Place a tangle of the sweet citrus on the side to enjoy with your dessert.

Step One
Preheat the oven to 350°F. Spray a 8" springform pan with nonstick cooking spray and line the bottom of the pan with a parchment round - coat with nonstick spray.

Step Two
Place the flour, baking powder, and zest in a bowl, stir to combine.

Step Three
In a large bowl, combine the yogurt, sugar, and eggs, stirring until well blended. Add the flour mixture to the yogurt mixture, then add the oil and stir to incorporate.

Step Four
Pour the batter into your prepared pan. Bake for 30-35 minutes, until the cake feels springy to the touch and a toothpick inserted into the center comes out clean. Cool the cake for 15 minutes.

Step Five
Run a knife around the edge of the pan, and remove it from the pan. With a toothpick poke holes all over the top. Combine the ingredients for the glaze and pour slowly over the cake. Cool completely before serving.

Tasty Wine Tip
Quady Orange Muscat Essensia, 375 ml (Half) Bottle  *California*
Total Wine about $17.00

This wine is often described as "Sunshine in a Glass". Made from the unusual Orange Muscat grape, it tastes like fresh oranges and caramel, balanced by good acidity. Pair a small glass with the Lemon Cake - or If you like your dessert wine fizzy, try adding it to sparkling water.

Toasted Pecan
Pumpkin Cake

*My family eats pumpkin all year round – not just at the holidays.
I especially like this cake recipe for two reasons: it tastes like
rich, moist, luscious pumpkin instead of just traditional pumpkin pie
spices AND it's since its made with canola oil instead of butter so we
are "eating better".*

Vegetarian

3 Large Eggs

1 15 oz Can Pumpkin

¾ Cup Canola or Vegetable Oil

½ Cup Water

1½ Cups All Purpose Flour

1 Cup Whole Wheat Pastry Flour

1 Cup Sugar

1 ¼ Cup Light Brown Sugar

1 ¼ Tsp Salt

1½ Tsp Baking Soda

1 Tsp Freshly grated Nutmeg

1 Tsp Cinnamon

1½ Cups toasted chopped Pecans

Taste and Savor TV: Toasting Nuts

Step One

Step One Preheat the oven to 350°F.
Grease and Flour, or use Baker's
Joy, a Bundt Pan.

Step Two

In a large bowl, whisk the
3 eggs. Add the pumpkin, oil and
water. Whisk until smooth. Add the
flours, sugars, salt, baking soda and
spices. Mix well. Stir in the nuts.

Step Three

Pour the batter into the pan, bake
65 to 75 minutes, or until
a toothpick inserted near the center
comes clean. Let cool on a rack for
10 minutes, remove from the pan
and let cool completely. If desired,
dust with powdered sugar.

Kitchen Smidgen

If you are not using Bakers Joy non stick spray - now is the time to start! With
no calories and no fat, it's an easy and light way to grease and flour pans in
one step.

get creative

And make Balsamic Baked Cranberries to top your cake - serve on the side with your Turkey Day bird - or just serve by itself with a dollop of marscapone, yogurt or whipped cream. To make this versatile side dish, start with an oven proof casserole dish. Add 4 cups fresh cranberries, 1 cup brown sugar, ¼ cup orange juice concentrate and the grated zest of an entire orange. Cover and bake in a 350°F oven for about 1 hour, or until cranberries are getting dark and bubbly. Remove from the oven and stir in ¼ cup Balsamic Vinegar.

Tasty Wine Tip

Erath Vineyards Pinot Noir   *Williamette Valley, Oregon*
Costco about $16.00

Pinot Noir, the noble grape of Burgundy gets my vote for the best Thanksgiving wine. It's fruit forward flavor and velvety smooth taste allow it to easily bridge the savory turkey and sides. For your big day try this American take on this noble grape: Oregon Pinot Noir. You'll find Erath has lovely blackberry and cherry flavors with a long clean finish-perfect for drinking from the appetizer through dessert.

Orange Fig Bars

*Did you grow up eating those fig bars in the yellow wrapper? I did.
And, just to let you know why it was my very favorite cookie – my
maiden name was Newton. So, I created this recipe to recreate my
childhood cookie memories – only better!*

Vegetarian

12 Ounces Dried Figs, chopped

¾ Cup Water

½ Cup Maple Syrup

2 TB grated Orange Zest

⅓ Cup Sugar

⅓ Cup Dark Brown Sugar

6 TB Butter, Softened

¾ Cup All Purpose Flour

¼ Cup Whole Wheat Flour

1 Cup Regular Oats

½ Tsp Baking Soda

¼ Tsp Salt

Non Stick Cooking Spray

Kitchen Smidgen

When measuring flour, never pack the measuring cup full. Always lightly spoon flour
into a dry measuring cup and level it with a knife. This method will ensure you
have just the right amount of flour for the recipe

get creative

To easily make the Orange Fig Bars dessert for guests, heat them in the microwave for about 30 seconds. Top them a dollop of Mascarpone Cheese - an Italian Cream Cheese. Garnish with a twist of orange.

Step One
Preheat the oven to 400°F. Spray a "9X9" square baking pan with non stick cooking spray.

Step Two
Combine the figs, water and maple syrup in a saucepan over medium heat. Bring to a boil, reduce the heat and cook and for 8-10 minutes or until most of the liquid is absorbed. Stir in the zest, set aside to cool.

Step Three
Cream the sugars and the butter with a mixer until smooth.

Step Four
In another bowl combine the flours, oats, baking soda and salt. Add the flour mixture to the sugar/butter mixture and stir to combine. (Mixture will be crumbly.)

Step Five
Press $2/3$ of the flour mixture into the bottom of the sprayed "9X9" pan. Spread the cooled fig mixture on top, and sprinkle with the remaining flour mixture. Bake for 25 to 30 minutes or until golden brown. Cool completely in the pan before cutting.

Tasty Wine Tip
Rosenblum Cellars Late Harvest, Rosie Rabbit Zinfandel  *California*
Whole Foods about $18.00

Wow! A flavorful, jammy dessert wine that is perfect for the fig bars - or divine just on its own. Rich, ripe raspberries and sweet dark cherries are apparent on the nose, and you'll taste the flavors of spicy strawberries and blackberry jam. Late harvest wines are exactly as they sound - grapes that have been left on the vines longer to develop more sugar, and the resulting wine is lush, rich and delicious!

Nutty Fruit Granola Bars

Crunchy, Sweet, Chewy, Satisfying...isn't that what we are all looking for in a snack bar? That's the reason for this recipe. As you all may know, I work a great deal with dieticians Shayna and Taryn to develop yummy foods that are also better eating. We had a cooking class, called "Food Sleuth" that was all about reading labels to find out just what is in the foods we eat often. Here's a quick recipe that doesn't require label reading! Subtly sweet from just a little sugar and dried fruit, it's also filled with nutty flavor.

 *Vegetarian*

1 Cup Raw Almonds

1 Cup Raw Pecans

3 Cups Oatmeal, divided

¼ Cup Whole Wheat Flour

1½ Cups chopped Dried Fruit

4 Large Eggs

½ Cup Dark Brown Sugar

2 TB Canola Oil

1½ Tsp Cinnamon

½ Tsp Allspice

½ Tsp Sea Salt

2 Tsp Vanilla Extract

Step One
Preheat the oven to 350°F Line a 9" x 13" pan with foil, allowing it to overhang from the sides. Coat with non-stick cooking spray.

Step Two
Place the nuts and the oatmeal on a large baking sheet with sides. Bake for 10 minutes or until toasted, stirring once. Chop finely in a food processor.

Kitchen Smidgen

Dates are a great choice for these bars. Did you know they come from a palm tree? Over 1500 date palm varieties are grown around the world. All parts of the tree have uses, from the leaves for Palm Sunday processions in Italy to building huts in North Africa. Humans are not the only species to eat dates - in the Sahara desert, dates are fed to camels, horses and dogs.

get creative

Did you know that by toasting the oatmeal we are making it crunchier and nutty tasting? Try this trick with your own recipe for oatmeal cookies — they will taste even better!

Step Three

Place the flour and 2 cups of the oatmeal in the processor and pulse until smooth. Combine with the dates, nuts and remaining cup of whole oatmeal.

Step Four

Whisk together the eggs, brown sugar, oil, cinnamon, allspice, salt, and vanilla extract in a large bowl. Stir in the oatmeal-almond mixture until well mixed. Spray your fingers with nonstick spray and pat the batter into the prepared pan.

Step Five

Bake for 30 minutes or until golden brown. Cool on a rack for an hour. Using the foil as handles, remove from the pan. Cut into bars with a serrated knife. To store for the week, wrap bars individually in plastic wrap and keep in the fridge.

Tasty Wine Tip

Bellini Vin Santo, (500 ml)  *Tuscany, Italy*
Total Wine about $25.00

In Italy they have a lovely afternoon custom of eating a small piece of not–too-sweet cake or biscotti with a tiny glass of Vin Santo. This break holds you over until a later dinner and definitely "perks" up conversation. You can embrace this ritual by enjoying a granola bar and a sip of this toffee flavored, nutty and honey tasting wine.

Feliz Navidads

I call these delicious cookies "Feliz Navidads" but even without the holiday season, you will get rave reviews for these yummy indulgences. My friend Carrie got a marriage proposal accompanied by Mexican Wedding Cookies. I used this recipe to recreate the moment – as a favor for her wedding guests!

Vegetarian

1 Cup Whole Wheat Pastry Flour

2 Cups Oats

1 Tsp Baking Soda

2 Tsp Cinnamon

1 Tsp Ground Allspice

½ Tsp Salt

1 Cup Canned Pumpkin

3 Eggs

½ Cup Canola Oil

2 Tsp Vanilla

1 Cup Dark Brown Sugar, packed

1 Cup chopped pitted Dates

1 Cup chopped toasted Pecans

Step One

Step One Preheat the oven to 400°F and line 2 baking sheets with parchment paper.

Step Two

Pour the oil into a medium bowl. Whisk the flours, ¼ cup of the confectioners sugar, the cornstarch and salt in another bowl.

Kitchen Smidgen

Cornstarch is more than just a thickener for gravy. Mixing cornstarch with flour essentially turns it into cake flour, which makes cakes and cookies lighter and more tender.

get creative

The name filbert is the correct name for the tree and nut. The name is of French origin and the tree was likely first introduced into the US by the French. Later, the English coined the name Hazelnut. Hazelnuts are rich in protein and unsaturated fat. They contain significant amounts of thiamine and B vitamins. Substitute hazelnuts for any other nuts in your baked goods for a punch of B power!

Step Three
Mix half the dry ingredients into the oil by large spoonfuls. Add the vanilla and then add the remaining dry ingredients by spoonfuls until thoroughly combined. Stir in the nuts.

Step Four
Roll the dough into 1" balls, place on the prepared baking sheets and bake until just set, 10 to 12 minutes. Cool for 2 minutes, and then transfer to a wire rack.

Step Five
Add the cinnamon to the remaining 1 ¾ cup powdered sugar and place in a pie plate, While the cookies are still warm, roll them in the sugar mixture. When completely cool roll them in he sugar again.

Taste and Savor TV: Toasting Nuts

Tasty Wine Tip
Rosa Regale d'Acqui, Italy
Total Wine about $17.00

If you are looking for a "cookie" wine - look no further - especially if your cookies contain chocolate! Rosa Regale is a frothy Italian wine made from the Brachetto grape in an area near Piedmont in Italy. It has luscious cherry-berry fruit flavors and an off-dry finish, and with only about 7% alcohol — makes it a great afternoon wine that won't knock you out for the rest of the day.

Triple Ginger and
Toasted Pecan Cookies

Loaded with ginger, these cookies are sweet and a little spicy and a perfect contrast to the luscious ice wine that I have suggested as a pairing. They are super with a cold glass of milk or an afternoon cup of tea, too!

 *Vegetarian*

⅔ Cup Sugar

⅓ Cup Unsalted Butter, softened

¼ Cup Blackstrap Molasses

1 Large Egg

1 TB Grated Fresh Ginger

1 Cup All-Purpose Flour

¾ Cup Whole Wheat Pastry Flour

¼ Cup finely chopped
   toasted Pecans

2 Tsp Baking Soda

1 Tsp Ground Ginger

2 Tsp + 3 TB finely ground
   Crystallized Ginger

3 TB Raw Sugar

Non-Stick Spray

Step One
Preheat oven to 350°F. Cream the sugar and butter with a mixer until fluffy. Add the molasses, egg and fresh ginger. Beat well.

Step Two
Combine flours, pecans, baking soda, and the ground and 2 Tsp crystallized ginger, in a bowl. Add the flour mixture to the sugar mixture. Stir until well blended. Divide the dough in half. Wrap each half in plastic wrap, and place in the refrigerator for at least 2 hours or overnight.

Step Three
Mix the 3 TB crystallized ginger and the raw sugar together. Place on a plate. Remove the dough from the refrigerator and roll into 1" balls; roll in ginger-sugar mixture on the plate. Place, 2" apart, on baking sheets coated with non-stick spray. Flatten a little with a fork dipped in the sugar. Bake at 350°F for 10-12 minutes or until lightly browned. Let cool on wire racks.

Kitchen Smidgen

Blackstrap molasses is a byproduct of the process of refining sugar cane into table sugar. Its dark bittersweet flavor adds a big punch of taste to these cookies as well as an excellent source of nutrients including iron.

get creative

Crystallized Ginger is fresh ginger that has been slowly cooked in sugar water and rolled in coarse sugar to preserve it. It may also be called candied ginger or glace ginger. For a gingery good treat try dipping crystallized ginger in melted dark chocolate.

 Taste and Savor TV: Toasting Nuts

Tasty Wine Tip

Kafer Eiswein  *Rheinhessen, Germany*
Total Wine about $20.00

It's hard to find an delicious ice wine in the $20 price range, but this golden colored one is a good value. Ice wine (Eiswein) is made with grapes that are picked and pressed when frozen, creating a very sweet or "luscious" dessert wine. (Ice wine is sweet, but should be balanced with a good acidity.) Kafer is medium bodied with a tropical flavor of apricots and peaches.

Decadent Dark Chocolate Brownies

A perfect day for me always includes chocolate. Most of the time, it's a couple of squares of really dark, good chocolate enjoyed with a cup of tea or coffee. But sometimes the brownie urge overtakes me, and I have to indulge. I've been working on this recipe for a couple of weeks now – and think I have nailed it. Dark and rich, moist and best of all, no fat! Pureed prunes add the texture that pull all the ingredients together.

 *Vegetarian*

1 Cup Whole Wheat Flour

½ Cup All Purpose Flour

1 Cup Unsweetened Cocoa Powder

1 TB Espresso Powder

1 Tsp Baking Powder

8 Egg Whites

14 pitted Prunes

½ Cup Reduced Fat Buttermilk

1 TB Vanilla Extract

1 Cup Dark Agave Syrup

1 Bar (3.5 oz) 60% (or More) Dark Chocolate, broken into small pieces

1 Cup Coarsely chopped toasted Walnuts

 Taste and Savor TV: Toasting Nuts

Kitchen Smidgen

It's amazing, but espresso powder actually brings out the dark cocoa flavors in chocolate. Instead of adding more sugar or fat for flavor, you can add espresso powder for deep rich chocolate desserts!

get creative

Light or Nonfat Buttermilk gives breads, brownies and cakes a tangy clean taste without adding much fat. And, it's an acidic ingredient, like yogurt and sour cream, so it helps tenderize the gluten in the batter, giving baked goods a softer texture.

Step One

Preheat the oven to 350°F. Line a 9" x 12" pan with parchment paper and lightly coat it with non-stick cooking spray.

Step Two

In a large bowl, whisk together the flours, cocoa, espresso powder and baking powder.

Step Three

In another bowl, whisk together egg whites until foamy; add the prunes, buttermilk, extract and agave. Pour it into the flour mixture and blend well. Stir in the chocolate.

Step Four

Spread the batter in the prepared pan and sprinkle with the walnuts. Bake 35 minutes or until a toothpick inserted near the center comes out with just a few crumbs. To prepare the prunes, soak them in 2 cups very hot tap water for 30 minutes, or until soft. Drain well, and puree in a food processor or blender. You need about ½ cup of pureed prunes for the recipe.

Tasty Wine Tip

NV Cockburn Fine Ruby Port *Portugal*
Total Wine about $13.00

Lots of chocolate treats taste delicious paired with a Ruby Port! The flavor of Cockburn's is often described as licorice and prunes with aromas of dark cherries and blackberries. Sweet and fruit forward, this three year old, matured in cask port, is a good example of the bright berry taste of a non vintage ruby port. Make sure to serve it slightly below room temp, 57-62°F. Because it's a fortified wine, (a ABV of 20%), the chill will knock out any harsh taste of alcohol.

Crunchy Orange
Oatmeal Cookies

These cookies make friends. Fast, easy and full of orange-y flavor, they are super for dessert, brown bag lunch or a bake sale.

Vegetarian

2 ¼ Cups Oatmeal
3 TBs Fresh Orange Juice
Zest of an Orange
½ Tsp Baking Powder
½ Tsp Baking Soda
¼ Tsp Salt
¼ Tsp Freshly grated Nutmeg
¼ Tsp Cinnamon
²⁄₃ Cup All Purpose Flour
⅓ Cup Whole Wheat Flour
3 TBs Unsalted Butter, Softened
3 TBs Canola Oil
1 Cup Dark Brown Sugar - Packed
1 Large Egg White
2 Tsp Vanilla Extract
¼ Cup Granulated or Raw Sugar

Preheat the oven to 350°F. Prepare 2 baking sheets with parchment paper or non-stick spray. Makes about 32 cookies.

Kitchen Smidgen

Do you know how to measure Brown Sugar correctly? It has lots of moisture, so it should be measured by packing it into a cup, then leveling off the top with the back of a knife. When you empty the cup, the sugar should stay in the shape of the cup.

get creative

Citrus Zest is a great idea for adding lots of flavor - without a lot of fat and calories. Next time the food you are cooking is a little blah - add the zest of a lemon to your dish. You will be surprised how good your food will taste!

Step One
Stir together the oats, oj and zest in a bowl and set aside.

Step Two
Stir together the next 7 ingredients - from the baking powder through the flour. Set aside.

Step Three
With a mixer, beat the butter and oil until well blended. Add the brown sugar, egg white and vanilla. Beat until smooth. Beat in the flour mixture - and then stir in the oatmeal mixture.

Step Four
Pitch off and roll the cookie dough into 1 inch balls. Flatten them with a glass dipped in the raw sugar. Bake the cookies for 8-10 minutes.

Tasty Wine Tip
La Veille Ferme Rose 🍇 *Cotes du Ventoux, France*
Cost Plus World Market about $9

This is definitely not your grandmother's pink wine - and it's perfect for a picnic or the grill. It's a light blend of 3 French grapes: Cinsault, Grenache and Syrah. Delicious and refreshing, it has wonderful strawberry and watermelon aromas and refreshing acidity.

Carrot Ginger Cake

One day I had a carrot cake craving. (What? Don't you have a carrot cake craving every once in a while?) I tested some of my old recipes to come up with one that was a little better for us. I think you will like the zing of the ginger, repeated 3 times with the use of ground ginger, fresh ginger and crystallized ginger.

Vegetarian

2 Cups Sugar

1 Cup Vegetable Oil

1 Cup All Purpose Flour

1 Cup Whole Wheat Flour

2 TB Baking Powder

1 Tsp Baking Soda

1 Tsp Salt

1 TB Cinnamon

1 TB Ground Ginger

4 Large Eggs

1 TB Fresh Ginger, grated

4 Cups grated Carrots

1 Cup chopped toasted Pecans

Step One
Preheat the oven to 350°F. Spray a bundt pan with non-stick Baking Spray.

Step Two
In the bowl of a mixer, combine the sugar and oil.

Step Three
Sift the flours, baking powder, baking soda, salt, cinnamon and ginger together. Add ½ of the mixture to the sugar and oil and beat on low speed to mix.

Step Four
Add the eggs and remaining flour in 4 batches, alternating flour then egg. Add in the fresh ginger, carrots and pecans. Bake for 1 hour or until a toothpick inserted in the cakes comes out clean.

Optional Glaze
Mix together 1 cup sugar and ¼ cup cornstarch in a saucepan. Add 1 cup orange juice and 1 TB lemon juice, then add 1 TB butter, zest from 1 orange and 2 TB chopped crystallized ginger. Cook and stir about 4 minutes. Let the glaze cool, pour over the cake and top with chopped toasted pecans.

Kitchen Smidgen

When adding nuts to a cake, toss them with a little flour before mixing them to your batter. It will keep them evenly distributed and stop them from dropping to the bottom.

get creative

Any recipe you make will get a big flavor boost with toasted nuts. Here's the best way to do it - without burning! Turn your oven on 350°F. Place the nuts on a sheetpan. After sliding them in the oven, set your timer for 8 minutes. Check the nuts - if they are done remove them. If not, set your timer for 2 more minutes - remove them when your timer goes off.

 Taste and Savor TV: Toasting Nuts

Tasty Wine Tip

Scharffenberger Brut Sparkling Wine   *California Mendocino County*
Total Wine about $20.00

If you are a fan of Scharffenberger chocolate - just wait til you try this wine. Made from $^2/_3$ Pinot Noir Grapes and $^1/_3$ Chardonnay, you'll discover a delicious aroma of strawberries and raspberries and a creamy rich tropical taste with a nice toasty finish.

taste and
savor life!

Acknowledgements

These pages just aren't big enough to hold the enormous gratitude I have for those who have helped me Taste and Savor my culinary passion.

Heartfelt Thanks to:

Mike, my husband who is also my biggest fan and supports me in every idea. Thank you for your patience and love with all the excitement that I seem to gather around me each day.

My parents who always told me I could do anything I wanted to do and my inspiring sister Pat, who shares my passion for food and wine and all things entertaining. Also to the awesome Gil, her husband.

My family has been unfailing with their compliments and encouragement. Van, Joyce, Mary, Beverly, Sam, Susan and Mike. My wonderful in-laws Jim and Sue and the guys and their families, especially Jim, Peter and Josie. My extended family of Alice, Daphna and Krista – I couldn't do it without you.

To my friends at Cancer Wellness at Piedmont, you are my new family. The incredible Manager Carolyn Helmer who was the instigator of this book and is my go-to for advice and support. Angela and Dennis, my encouragers and teachers of all things good; Rebecca who helps me stretch not only my body but my mind; Amy with the beautiful spirit who knows exactly what to say; sage Jackie who keeps me sane and is the best listener in the world and my friend David who not only needles me, but shares insights as well. Shayna, who shares my passion for eating well and her expertise; Sarah who always spurs me on and Mendal who has such confidence in me, thank you. The rest of the incredibly talented staff, Director John Goodman, Dr. Jody, Cindy, Barbara, Tallulah, Taryn, Tavari, Edna and Arrington, you are friends who are always there to provide assistance and most of all love. Tawyna and Kim, you make it

all run perfectly; interns Julie, Daniel and Tyler who have been great sports and lots of fun, and to all my many marvelous friends that are way too many to name – you have changed my life. A note to my wonderful sangha on Thursday mornings, you all are my constant companions and buoy me up each and every day. Thank you, thank you, thank you.

Fantastic Donna Brown, my roomie and oldest friend; and of course the terrific Becky who is the third in our trio of trouble. Many thanks go Connie my restaurant buddy and lover of the good life; Carrie my fashionesta friend and her wonderful sister, the positive Dr. Laura Mixon. To Flo and Jack and Rebecca and Peter some of the most caring and authentic friends I have ever had. For Cheryl my greatest listening friend and Mike who saved me from myself many times. Marilyn, my most glamorous buddy; Beautiful Lisa, often my inspiration; Susan, my compatriot in learning and growing; Lynn, not only a walking but a sharing friend; Beci, one of the most amazing and caring women I have ever met; Elizabeth, the most creative and best connector in the world; Jack and Kathy who are great encouragers; Kelly my good wine friend; Sue my intrepid UK roomie; Frank, who is a morale booster and my brain doppelganger; Mary Nell who is always interesting and inspiring; Janet who always makes me laugh and all the other great pals too numerous to name, that I have met during my travels.

I couldn't have charted my own path without help from Mary Moore, owner of Cooks Warehouse, Cooley Fales, the former cooking school director and the current director, wonderful Wendy Allen. Chefs Virginia and Gena - thank you so much for having confidence in me from the very beginning. I couldn't teach a single class without the absolutely incredible Cooks Warehouse assistants, Yinka, Tonya, Kizee, Mary, Elise, Ashley, Alison, Joanne and the other ace cooking school assistants and leads plus

Acknowledgements

the outstanding crew of store managers like David and Matt, office staff like Simone and Gregg and other fantastic employees. A special shout out to the Taste Club team of Renee, Brenda, Julie and Julie, Matt, Jennifer and Katie – you all make sharing a Saturday night each month such a good time.

Kristin Sharma and I have shared many curries and commiserated on the challenges of owning our own business. And for Chef Hans Rueffert who always sees the bright side and never ever gives up, special thanks. The incredibly talented and hard working Tiffany Thompson makes me look good in the kitchen and on in cyberspace, Cyndi who is always there for me and Tracy who swoops in and takes care of business. Beth Phillips, one of the greatest inspirations around and the rest of the Piedmont Fayette Ladies Auxiliary who are always there to help, eat and laugh. And, to the lovely Lydia, Laurie and Nina who just smile at my foibles and work really, really hard.

My thanks could not be complete without recognizing the incredible doctors who have been my guides though cancer. Your dedication, professionalism and caring inspire me everyday. Bill Barber, Eric Minniberg, Fred Schwaibold and Joe Woods, thank you for putting me back together and making me strong.

This book couldn't have been done without the inimitable Nancy Sherrill, designer extraordinaire. Thank you for your patience, kindness and all your help. Cheers to this one just being the start of wonderful things to come. Printer Greg Daney at PCG-ATL Studios made Taste and Savor rock! And thanks go to all the wonderful photographers like Lynn Stowe, Jennifer Gantner, Brenda Hill, Renee Jackson, Sean Bolt and Grace Natoli Sheldon whose fantastic pictures have made my food and memories come alive.

TASTE and SAVOR TV

http://www.youtube.com/user/tasteandsavortv.com

Here's a list of the current culinary "shorts" appearing on Taste and Savor TV. Check back often at LINK to discover new videos that will help you learn how to cook faster and better!

Chopping and Seeding Tomatoes
Chopping Herbs
Chopping Onions
Cutting Chicken
Cutting a Mango
Grating Garlic and Ginger
Making Salad Dressing
Peeling and Chopping Avocados
Roasting Peppers
Toasting Nuts
Using Chiles
Using a Mandoline

favorite links

For help and information about cancer wellness programs, go to
www. piedmontcancer.org

The link www.livingandeatingwell.com is my collaboration with Dietician
Shayna Komar on quick, easy and healthy recipes and super nutrition information.

If you are a young women with cancer, or know someone who is,
visit www.pinkheals.org for help, advice, and connection.

Ensure your Indian food is authentic and delicious by visiting
www.moderndaymasala.com

Using fresh herbs is easier when you visit Shenandoah Growers website
www.freshherbs.com for recipes and tips.

Visit the Mixonian Institute when you need a lift at www.mixonian.com

For local food in season it can't be better than my friend prepares -
Chef Hans Rueffert, owner of the Woodbridge Inn at www.hanscooks.com

Check out my super web designer, Robert Brown at www.McKinleyBrown.com

My friend Nancy at Shine Design Studioa can help you with your next project at
www.shinedesignstudios.com

Greg Daney at www.pgc-atl.com will shepherd your printing project from start
to finish.

Acupuncturist David Hobbs is knowledgeable, compassionate and friendly at
www.hobbsacupuncture.com

Every
with
Marcus
& Lisa
Day

WEEKDAYS
11 AM – 12 PM ET

EveryDay Home

Meet Marcus and
Lisa Ryan

Guest Guide

Featured Videos

Photo Gallery

Recipes

Resources

Contact EveryDay

Watch FamilyNet on

TVU
networks

Play

TODAY on EVERYDAY

Micah Linton
Kid's Hunger for Learning

Carri Taylor
Children of Divorce

Nancy Waldeck
Taste and Savor

View Full Guest Guide

Recipes

FEATURED on EVERYDAY

Nancy Waldeck
Taste and Savor

Crisp and Crunch Apple Salad
Spinach Salad with Cashews and Chutney Dressing

BEHIND THE SCENES

EXPLORE THE SITE

CONTACT   HOME

Fresh Flavors / The Friday Four / Wonderful Wine / Blog

Necessary Things / Food, Beautiful Food / What is Taste and Savor

Taste and Savor
by Nancy Waldeck

Welcome to
Taste and Savor
You're in the right place
to find fun, fresh food
ideas and wine tips that
you can really use!

Discover simple strategies for living better -
recipes with minimum fuss and maximum
satisfaction PLUS new ways to enjoy wine. Here
are the resources to help you everyday in the
kitchen using straightforward recipes and
seasonal ingredients in a way that suits them
best. This passion for food and wine is
contagious! Click in and explore how Taste and
Savor can help you accomplish your culinary
goals.

*Curious about
what's on our mind*
READ OUR IDEAS AND SHARE YOURS AT OUR BLOG
GO →

Focus on the chef
ALL ABOUT NANCY WALDECK   GO →

Taste and Savor
Kitchen and Pantry Staples

Here's a list of the ingredients that you will want to stock up on when you are planning to cook through the book.

Spices

Smoked Paprika is a popular ingredient in many Mediterranean recipes. Once you try it you'll use it again and again. Made from smoked, ground pimiento peppers, it has awesome savory flavor tastes great on just about everything. If you are a vegetarian or limiting your intake of meat, try smoked paprika for a "bacon-y" taste. Find it in the spice section of your grocery store.

Turmeric is a yellow-colored power pack of antioxidants. Not only does it turn your food a beautiful saffron color, it also helps fight inflammation. MD Anderson Hospital is currently conducting clinical trials on turmeric. When you use it in cooking, make sure to warm it in a little oil with black pepper. You'll increase the bioavailability of all its good-for-you ingredients.

Ground Chiles from Ancho to Chipotle, help ramp up the flavor in food without necessarily adding lots of heat. Try buying your own ground chilies to make your own Chile Powder blends by adding cumin, salt and pepper.

Garam Masala is a spice I can't do without. Just like curry powder it is a blend of spices that is unique to each household. Made from ingredients like cumin, cardamom, nutmeg, cinnamon, anise and black peppercorns it is pungent, but not hot. My favorite brand is my Modern Day Masala, but any national brand will do in a pinch.

Italian Seasoning and Herbes de Provence are both herb blends from the beautiful Mediterranean. Similar ingredients are basil, thyme, marjoram and oregano. Often herbes de Provence also includes dried orange peel and lavender. If you don't have one of them, you can substitute the other with no loss in quality of your final dish.

Sea Salt is just what it sounds like, salt obtained by the evaporation of seawater. Because of its mineral content, it may taste a little different than table or kosher salt. When cooking, I prefer to use coarse ground sea salt and with baking my choice is fine ground sea salt.

Freshly Ground Black Pepper is a must for good cooking. If you have pre-ground black pepper at home, open up the tin and smell the difference between it and some freshly ground pepper. Now you understand what I am talking about. If you get tired of grinding all the time, every few days take a TB of peppercorns and process them in your spice grinder. Put them in a bowl on your counter and you will quickly discover what a difference the fresh pungent pepper can make in your cooking.

Condiments

Dijon Mustard is made with brown or black mustard seeds that are zestier and more full flavored than the yellow seeds. I use Dijon in lots of recipes, not only for its taste but its ability to emulsify ingredients in dressings and sauces.

Mayonnaise with Olive Oil is now available and easy to find. Soybean oil is used in most prepared mayos – mainly because it is cheap. Recently Kraft released a mayo made with olive oil with reduced fat. It's a super alternative to other mayos on the market.

Capers are the unripe buds of a plant native to the Mediterranean. After the buds are harvested, they are dried in the sun, then pickled in vinegar or salt. Curing brings out their tangy flavor, similar to olives. Capers pickled in vinegar are easy to find, and perfect for Taste and Savor recipes.

Calamata, (Kalamata) olives are from Greece, and named for the city around which the olives are grown. They are especially fruity tasting with a meaty texture. Their unique flavor is enhanced by the vinegar marinade that they are often soaked in. I love the convenience of having sliced and pitted Kalamata olives in the pantry.

Vegetables

Canned Tomatoes are a staple I can't live without. Muir Glen from California makes my favorite brand. Try the fire-roasted tomatoes for an extra boost of flavor.

Canned Beans are often my go-to on hectic weeknights or leisurely weekends. I have a row each of Cannellini, Garbanzo and Black Beans in my Pantry. As long as you rinse and drain them well, they are a super substitute for home made.

Canned Pumpkin is one of my favorite ingredients for dessert, soups and any dish that needs creamy texture and light sweet flavor. I actually prefer canned pumpkin to fresh – too often fresh is stringy and lacks taste.

Grains, Pasta and Rice

Whole Wheat Pasta is made from made from 100 percent whole durum wheat (the same high-protein variety that's refined for use in the best white pastas). The key to making good whole wheat pasta is to NOT overcook it. Leave it "al dente" or just a little firmer than white pasta – it will be nutty and delicious. Trying to get used to whole wheat pasta is easy. Just incorporate a quarter, then a half of whole wheat pasta to the white pasta you are used to eating. By the time you are eating three quarters of the whole wheat pasta – you will have switched.

Whole Wheat Couscous is not a grain but a pasta. It can be made of barley, corn or semolina, but whole wheat couscous tastes nutty and toasty. Tiny grains of pasta make a quick and easy base that acts like a sponge, soaking up any delicious flavors you add.

Grains, Pasta and Rice

Quinoa (Keen-wah) contains all 9 essential amino acids, making it a power packed protein source. Most commonly considered a grain, quinoa is actually a relative of leafy green vegetables like spinach and Swiss chard. Revered by the Incas as the "mother grain" it is actually a seed from the Goosefoot plant. Sold in the U.S. only since the mid-eighties, it has a mild nutty flavor that is a great background for strong bold flavors like smoked paprika, lemon juice and garlic.

Try substituting Quinoa for Couscous or Rice in your favorite dish.

Brown Basmati Rice is the healthier version of deliciously fragranced Basmati rice. Basmati has longer grains than other rices, making it easy to cook and keep warm without becoming sticky. Brown rice is unmilled, chewier and more nutritious than white rice.

Sweeteners and Flours

Pomegranate Molasses is simply reduced pomegranate juice. It has a unique, tart-sweet flavor and is a gorgeous red jewel color. Use it in anything calling for honey or molasses, or put a teaspoon in your tea. If your local store don't carry it, it's easily found on the web.

Agave Nectar or Syrup is a sweetener produced in Mexico from the same plant as tequila. I like it for 2 reasons: it is sweeter than sugar, so I can use less of it in a recipe and it has less of a glycemic load so you don't get as much of a sugar rush when eating it. When you replace the sugar in a recipe with agave make sure you only use half of the amount of sugar called for in the recipe. Be aware that agave will create a more "cakey" texture than regular sugar.

Stevia is an herb plant from the sunflower family. It has recently been approved for sale in the United States as a sweetener. It is 300 times sweeter than sugar, so just a pinch will make your food sweet

Whole Wheat Pastry Flour allows you to add extra nutrition to any of your baked goods without sacrificing flavor or texture. Not all of the bran and germ portions of the wheat kernel have been removed during the milling process, so it has a fine-texture and a high starch content perfect for baking.

Chocolate is an essential ingredient in my pantry - how about yours? In order to make your chocolate not only delicious, but good for you too, keep in mind these two tips. First, look for chocolate that is 70% or more cocoa solids. This means the sweet treat will have more flavonoids than lower percentage chocolate. Flavonoids in chocolate act as antioxidants that protect the body from aging caused by free radicals. Second, make sure your bar does not have either "dutch processed" or "processed with alkali" in the ingredients list. When chocolate is treated with alkali or dutch processed, many of the flavonoids are removed.

Vinegars and Oils

Balsamic Vinegar is prized for its sweet, fruity flavor and mild acidity. You can use it in everything from appetizers to dessert. Expensive artisan-made balsamic vinegars are aged in wood barrels for at least 12 years and can cost over $100 per bottle. No need to mortgage the house for the recipes in this cookbook, commercially available Balsamic is fine.

Sherry Vinegar is Spain's answer to Italy's Balsamic. Made from Sherry, it's smooth yet potent and assertive, a tangy alternative to try with almost any Mediterranean dish. Both sherry (the wine) and the vinegar have been produced in southern Spain since well before the 16th century.

Rice Vinegar is sweeter, milder, and less acidic than Western vinegars, 4% acidity versus average 6% in other vinegars. This makes it a great alternative for those undergoing treatment for illness, individuals who don't like acidic foods or simply as an ingredient in a delicious salad dressing that won't compete with your wine. You may hear the term "rice wine" vinegar – it refers to the way the vinegar has been processed – but it is exactly the same as rice vinegar. Make sure to buy the unseasoned variety.

Extra Virgin Olive Oil is my oil of choice. Olive oils that are less than 1% acidity and produced by the first pressing of the olive fruit through the cold pressing process are called extra-virgin olive oil. You don't have to spend a lot of money on this oil, most commercially available oils are fine for cooking. To finish a dish, or make a special salad dressing, its fun to taste oils from different countries to decide on your favorite.

Toasted or Dark Sesame Oil is an excellent addition to any dish that for which you want to a pop of deep dark nutty taste. This dark colour and flavor are derived from roasted/toasted sesame seeds. Cold pressed sesame oil has a different flavour than the toasted oil, its often used in Indian versus other Asian cuisines. Make sure to add the sesame oil at the end of your preparation, when you add it during cooking it loses some of its delicious taste.

Nut Oils – Roasted Almond, Walnut, and Hazelnut are the perfect enhancers when you are looking for an alternative to olive oil. Just like toasted sesame oil, nut oils are best as finishers: as a drizzle over a piece of grilled fish or chicken, or as an ingredient in a sauce or delicious dressing. Make sure to store open nut oils in the fridge – they are delicate and can go rancid easily.

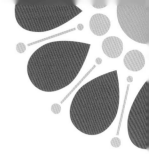

Four Easy Steps to Taste Wine

I like to think of appreciating and learning about wine as a four-step process. For me, it's easiest to remember when I use the parts of my face as a guide.

Eyes: Check out the color of the wine. Is it yellow? Gold? Ruby? Garnet? Does it have a hint of brown around the edges? Can you see through the wine? Wine color is a clue to the variety of grape, as well as age and body. White wine tends to get darker and browner as it ages, and red wine tends to lighten up.

Nose: Here's your chance to swirl and name the flavors in the wine. Even "it smells like grapes" counts as a descriptor for the wine's fragrance. Exclaiming "yum!" does not. Try to use words that everyone will identify with. It's easiest to think of wine's aroma as a type of fruit, flower, herb or spice, nut, type of wood, metal, rock or ground.

Mouth: Finally we get to taste the wine! Does it taste the way it smells? What's different? Let the wine run down on either side of the back of your tongue to check out the acidity. Acidity is good in wine, as long as it is balanced. Acidity keeps the wine from tasting flabby or too sweet. As a general rule, high acidity indicates cooler growing regions, low acid wines come from warmer areas. Run the wine under your front lip to see how much tannin is in a wine. The fuzzier your teeth feel, the more tannins a wine has – tannins are created from the grape seeds, stems, skins, pits and during ageing when wood comes in contact with the wine. They act as a preservative, and give wine structure, texture and flavor.

Chin: Now for the finish, or how long the wine stays in your mouth. A wine doesn't necessary need to linger in your mouth a long time. If you are on the porch enjoying a light cool summer white, you want the finish to float away so you are ready for the next sip. Heavy wines with lots of body and tannins tend to hang around longer. Think of a hefty Cabernet with a juicy chop. Wine like this can go on and on, the better to enjoy the hardy food accompaniment.

If you take just a few minutes to record your reflections in a wine journal, you will soon discover exactly how to explain and share the wonderful world of wine.

Chef Nancy Waldeck
believes that Good Food
doesn't have to be hard.

Chef Nancy Waldeck discovered this simple truth early in life. Growing up in a family who not only traveled the world, but ate it too, she discovered her appetite for all things culinary. Ultimately, looking for every opportunity to throw a party just wasn't enough - Her aha! moment occurred in 2000 when she decided her passion for food and wine couldn't wait. It was scary, but she charted her own path, pursued it with enthusiasm and enjoyed every step of the way.

Always a healthy eater with a love of exercise, she became more so when she was diagnosed with breast cancer a few years ago. Now she takes food seriously and has embarked on a journey to understand the science behind healthy eating. She loves teaming up with forward-thinking dieticians and other professionals to share the most current information with her classes.

A zeal for wine and food pairing led to an advanced certification from London's Wine and Spirits Education Trust. Interesting wine and food classes, compelling writing, innovative health-supportive recipe development and accomplished media work are all part of her culinary portfolio. From working on the Turner South show, Home Plate, to monthly appearances on the nationally syndicated morning show, Everyday with Marcus and Lisa, from classes for Cancer Wellness to instructing other chefs at the American Embassy in Africa, Nancy has taken her passion for good food and delicious wine across the world.

As a chef and breast cancer survivor, she believes that food should be fast, fun, healthy AND taste great. Every week you can connect with Nancy and her friends as she translates food from ordinary to healthy in The Friday Four e-zine.

Go to www.tasteandsavor.com to join in the experience.

228